Eldad's Travels: A Journey from the Lost Tribes to the Present

In the latter years of the ninth century, a mysterious figure arrived in the North African Jewish community of Kairouan. The visitor, Eldad of the tribe of Dan, claimed to have arrived from the kingdom of the Israelite tribes whose whereabouts had been lost for over a millennium and a half. Communicating solely in Hebrew, the sojourner's vocabulary contained many words that were unfamiliar to his hosts. This enigmatic traveler not only baffled and riveted the local Jewish community but has continued to grip audiences and influence lives into the present era.

This book takes stock of the long journey that both Eldad and his writings have made through Jewish and Christian imaginations from the moment he stepped foot in North Africa to the turn of the new millennium. Each of its chapters assays a major leg of this voyage, offering an in-depth look at the original source material and shedding light on the origins and later reception of this elusive character.

Micha J. Perry is a historian of medieval history at the department of Jewish History at the University of Haifa.

T0386340

Eldad's Travels: A Journey from the Lost Tribes to the Present

Micha J. Perry

Routledge
Taylor & Francis Group

LONDON AND NEW YORK

First published 2019 by Routledge

2 Park Square, Milton Park, Abingdon, Oxon OX14 4RN

605 Third Avenue, New York, NY 10017

Routledge is an imprint of the Taylor & Francis Group, an informa business

First issued in paperback 2021

Copyright © 2019 Micha J. Perry

The right of Micha J. Perry to be identified as author of this work has been asserted by him in accordance with sections 77 and 78 of the Copyright, Designs and Patents Act 1988.

All rights reserved. No part of this book may be reprinted or reproduced or utilised in any form or by any electronic, mechanical, or other means, now known or hereafter invented, including photocopying and recording, or in any information storage or retrieval system, without permission in writing from the publishers.

Notice:
Product or corporate names may be trademarks or registered trademarks, and are used only for identification and explanation without intent to infringe.

Publisher's Note

The publisher has gone to great lengths to ensure the quality of this reprint but points out that some imperfections in the original copies may be apparent.

British Library Cataloguing in Publication Data
A catalogue record for this book is available from the British Library

Library of Congress Cataloging-in-Publication Data
Names: Perry, Micha, 1972- author.
Title: Eldad's travels : a journey from the lost tribes to the present / Micha Perry.
Description: First edition. | London ; New York, NY : Routledge/ Taylor & Francis Group, 2019. | Includes bibliographical references and index.
Identifiers: LCCN 2018041105| ISBN 9781138368354 (hardback) | ISBN 9780429429309 (e-book)
Subjects: LCSH: Eldad, ha-Dani, active 9th century. | Lost tribes of Israel. | Jews--Travel--History.
Classification: LCC DS131 .P45 2019 | DDC 909/.04924--dc23
LC record available at https://lccn.loc.gov/2018041105

ISBN: 978-1-138-36835-4 (hbk)
ISBN: 978-1-03-217843-1 (pbk)
DOI: 10.4324/9780429429309

Typeset in Times New Roman
by Taylor & Francis Books

Dedicated to my parents, Chaim and Shuli Peri

Contents

Preface

In approximately 884 CE, a man claiming to have arrived from the land of the Tribe of Dan showed up in the Jewish community of Kairouan, a city in present-day Tunis. Going by the name Eldad, this mysterious visitor spoke exclusively in the holy tongue, which he spiced with words unknown to the local Jews. Moreover, the guest told the members of Kairouan's Jewish community incredible stories about the Ten Tribes. According to his testimony, the Lost Tribes are scattered throughout the four corners of the Earth. For instance, he claimed that Levites known as *bnei Moshe* (sons of Moses) were hemmed in by the *Sambation* River – a stream that flings sand and gargantuan rocks six days a week, while resting on the Sabbath. What is more, Eldad disclosed a unique tradition of animal slaughter (*shechitat ḥulin*). Unlike the Rabbinic literature, these laws did not cite the names of sages. Instead, each division opened with the following words: "Our rabbi Joshua said in the name of Moses in the name of the Almighty." Baffled by the discrepancies between the sojourner's teachings and their own laws, the Kairouan community dispatched a query to R. Zemaḥ ben Ḥayim, the gaon of Sura (served 889–895), a version of which has survived into the modern era. There are also existing stories attributed to Eldad on the Ten Tribes and a letter featuring hair-raising, Sinbad-like tales. This material excited the Jewish world by rekindling the hitherto latent myth of the Lost Tribes residing in a fantastical land where they are patiently waiting for the right moment to spring into action and rescue their brethren in the Diaspora. Eldad's image, stories, and writings continued to make the rounds in both the Jewish and non-Jewish world. As we shall see, the staying power of these traditions over the length of medieval and modern Jewish civilization makes for a riveting narrative in its own right.

The present book endeavors to shed light on the image of Eldad the Danite. All the more so, it will reconstruct the transmission of his story and the texts that he putatively wrote. In the chapters to come, these

works are read through the lens of dichotomous poles and key milestones in Jewish history and its entanglement with crossing histories. In
this journey I will follow in the footsteps of Alain Boureau, a French
historian who unearthed past incarnations of various myths, like that
of Pope Joan or *jus primae noctis* ("the right of the first night"), and
assessed their impact on European society.[1] Employing Boureau's
methods, this undertaking reconstructs the transmission and reception
of Eldad's narratives. The book opens with an introduction to the life
and times of this puzzling figure (chapter 1). In chapter 2, I will grapple
with the historical question of whether Eldad even existed and if he was
indeed a member of the Ten Tribes? The third chapter explores the myth
of the Tribes: the ideals and hopes that it spread throughout the Exile.
Chapters 4 and 5 revolve around the "Talmud" of the Lost Tribes that
Eldad unveiled. Correspondingly, we will place this story within its
immediate, contemporaneous contexts: the disputes between the Karaites and Rabbinites and between the Land of Israel and Babylonian
Jewish communities. At this point, the spotlight shifts to the role that
Eldad's stories played in male–female (chapter 6) and Jewish–Christian
(chapter 7) relations. The final chapter surveys how Eldad helped
Ethiopian Jewry gain entry into the Jewish community at large. For that
aim it unveils a shared discourse by rabbis, adventurers, ethnographers,
and critical scholars from the sixteenth to the twentieth centuries.

I have no pretenses of exhausting the topic of the Ten Tribes or, for
that matter, the story of Eldad. In fact, this book has readily eschewed
important aspects of these fields. A case in point is the search for the
Lost Tribes in the 1500s against the backdrop of Columbus' discovery
of the "New World."[2] My decision to forego these topics stems in part
from two of the work's other goals: to present some major literature
and themes in medieval Jewish history; and to open a window onto the
historian's craft. At the outset, the book adopts a philological
approach, the main tool of the positivist approach, whereupon we shift
the focus to political, social, cultural, and gender history. That said,
our overarching subject is the annals of the transmission and reception
of texts as well as their historical and social contextualization. By this,
we are less interested in finding the "origins" of the Eldad literature or
the man himself. Instead, the book leans more toward explicating the
sundry readings of that same "original" (text, story, or tradition) and
its metamorphosis over the ages. These developments can either be
textual and contextual or ex-textual: pertaining to the readers' interpretation. The findings indicate that these changes are not "mistakes"
or "distortions," but the source, as well as the tradition it represents,
was adapted (be it deliberately or unconsciously) to suit the needs of

the present. In charting these developments, I aspire to expand the purview of the historical analysis of texts and ideas beyond the single author to society at large by gauging the literature's impact on its expansive audience and examining its disparate meanings.[3]

Finally, an essential part of this book is the direct, personal encounter with the historical sources themselves. To this end, each chapter opens with excerpts from pertinent sources, allowing the reader to enjoy their richness, as well as the ability to judge my own readings and conclusions.

Notes

1 Alain Boureau, *The Myth of Pope Joan*, tr. Lydia G. Cochrane (Chicago 2001); idem, *The Lord's First Night*, tr. Lydia G. Cochrane (Chicago 1998).
2 The most insightful recent study on these topics is: Zvi Ben-Dor Benite, *The Ten Lost Tribes: A World History* (Oxford 2009). See as well: Moti Benmelech, *Shlomo Molcho: The Life and Death of Messiah Ben Joseph* (Jerusalem 2016), 33–49 [Hebrew]. An upcoming book by my friends and colleagues, Alexandra Cuffel and Adam Knobler, is aimed to serve as a comprehensive history of the myth of Ten Lost Tribes.
3 See the introduction to my book; Micha Perry, *Tradition and Transformation: Knowledge Transmission among European Jews in the Middle Ages* (Bnei Brak 2010) [Hebrew].

Acknowledgments

The work on this book was done through the generosity of a G.I.F. Grant (no. I-1279–111.4/2014) titled: "The Ten Lost Tribes: A Cross-Cultural Approach." A longer version of chapter 7 was previously published as: "The Imaginary War between Prester John and Eldad the Danite and Its Real Implications," in: *Viator* 41/1 (2010): 1–23.

This book brings together different instances, over a decade and several continents, I have worked on Eldad and his texts. Though I am grateful to them infinitely, trying to name all the friends, colleagues, teachers, and librarians who helped me along the way will burden this introduction and certainly leave someone out. Briefly I will only thank my colleagues at Haifa University; the librarians at the National Library of Israel; my teacher and mentor, Robert Bonfil; Avi Aronsky, who translated most of this book and edited all of it; last, special thanks to my family: my parents to whom I dedicate the work, parents-in-law, brothers, sisters-in-law, and above all: Sandra, Shira, Hillel, and Tuvia.

1   Query and response

The Kairouan community's query to R. Zemaḥ ben Ḥayim:

> We wish to inform our master that a man by the name of Eldad the
> Danite from the tribe of Dan visited our community. He told us that
> four tribes – Dan, Naphtali, Gad, and Asher – are in one place:
> ancient Evilas, where the gold is. They have a judge by the name of
> Abadun, and they pass judgement on [cases involving] the four
> capital punishments. Residing in tents, they travel from place to place
> and set up camp. They [are immersed in] battle with the seven kings
> of Kush. It takes seven months to traverse their land, and five of
> those same kings, with whom they are constantly at war, surround
> them from the backside and two flanks. Whoever is faint-hearted is
> placed at the service of God. Although they possess the [Hebrew]
> Bible in its entirety, they read from neither the scroll of Esther's
> deeds, for they were not involved in that same miracle, nor the Scroll
> of Lamentations, lest their heart be broken. Throughout their
> Talmud, there is no [mention of] any sage, but rather "Joshua said in
> the name of Moses [who said] in the name of the Almighty." Every
> man of strength is put to war, and they do not budge from their post.
> Upon their induction, they do not mobilize in mixed units. The war-
> riors of Dan have three months of fixed duty. They chase their foes on
> their horses and do not dismount all week long. On the eve of the
> Sabbath, they dismount wherever they happen to be, and their horses
> stand with the arms of warfare. If their foes do not confront them,
> they rest on Sabbath in accordance with the law; and if their enemies
> do attack, they set forth with all their arms and slay many of them as
> the courage of the Holy One imbues them. Within their ranks are
> brave men from amongst the sons of Samson and Dalilah, who run
> to engage their foes in battle. The smallest among them will chase
> many, and each of them shouts the battle cry loud as the roar of the

lion: "To God shall be the victory! May Your courage be imparted to Your nation, the tribes of Jeshurun, *selah.*" And they battle in war until the three months are over, whereupon they come with all the booty to King Adiel and he divides everything up evenly among all the Israelites. Upon receiving his portion, the king gives it to the sages studying Torah. Whoever is worthy, gets a portion. And the same can be said for [the three months rotation of] Gad, Asher, and Naphtali until the twelve months are complete, and then it [i.e., the annual cycle] is repeated.

They have no other language, but the Holy Tongue. This Eldad the Danite does not understand so much as a single utterance in either the language of Kush or the language of Ishmael [i.e., African languages and Arabic], only the Holy Tongue. Moreover, the holy language that he speaks contains words that we never heard. For instance, he calls a dove a *tintara*, a bird a *riqut*, and peppers a *darmosh.* We wrote down many examples of the words that he used. After showing him an item, he told us its name in the Holy Tongue and we wrote it down; days later, we returned and asked [Eldad to repeat the name] of each and every item, and we found that it was the same as before. Their Talmud is [composed] in eloquent Holy Tongue. There is no mention of any sage, either from the Mishna or the Talmud; instead, the following is stated in every passage: "Thus we learnt from the mouth of Joshua, [who learnt] from the mouth of Moses, [who learnt] from the mouth of the Almighty." And in telling us what is forbidden and permitted in dietary laws, we came to the realization that the Torah [we share] is one, albeit with a few changes. And we found it necessary to send before his eminence [i.e., R. Zemaḥ] a modicum of which we have written from their Talmud, for as you shall see, it arouses great wonder.[1]

We have opened this introductory chapter with the first part of a legal question concerning one Eldad the Danite. The query was dispatched by the Jewish community in Kairouan, a city in modern-day Tunis, to Rabbi Zemaḥ ben Ḥayim, the gaon (head of the major Torah academy, *yeshiva*) in Babylonia, whom sent back his response. Both of these letters are bound together and preserved as part of the Responsa literature (*she'ailot u'tshuvot*) – a prevalent Jewish genre since the Middle Ages. Before delving into this particular exchange, let us briefly set the historical backdrop.

As chronicled in the Hebrew Bible, King Shalmaneser V of Assyria captured the Kingdom of Samaria – the home of the Ten Tribes – in approximately 772 BCE. Thereafter, he "deported the Israelites to Assyria and settled them in Halah, at the [River] Habor, at the River

Gozan, and in the towns of Media ... So the Israelites were deported from their land to Assyria, as is still the case" (II Kings 17:6, 23). Their co-religionists and erstwhile neighbors from the Kingdom of Judah (the tribes of Judah and Benjamin, along with Levites) lost contact with the Israelites. By the opening centuries of the Common Era, there were disputes among the rabbis over the fate of these exiles:

> The Ten Tribes are not destined to return, for it is said: 'And cast them off to another land, as is this day'. Just as the day goes and does not return, so too they went and will not return; this is R. Akiva's view. R. Eliezer said: 'As this day' – just as the day darkens and then becomes light again, so too the Ten Tribes: even as it went dark for them, so too will it become light for them (*Mishna*, tractate Sanhedrin, chap. x, §3).

From this point forward, the Lost Tribes quickly began to dominate the narrative of apocalyptic visions. A case in point is *IV Esdras* – a messianic book of uncertain provenance. More specifically, scholars disagree over whether to categorize this work as Jewish, Christian, both, or originally Jewish with a Christian ending. In any event, *IV Esdras* describes the Ten Tribes as an army that is destined to accompany the messiah (Jesus) and punish the sinners.

Other elements, which as we will see below (chapter 3) were incorporated into Eldad's account, also appear at this time. The Sambation River makes its debut in Flavius Josephus' *The Jewish War* (book 31, chapter 8). The sages offer two different pictures of this mythical waterway. One is of a river whose marvels demonstrate that the Sabbath is the natural day of rest (e.g., *Genesis Rabbah*, p. 11). In this rendering, the river's magical properties are less conspicuous; and it apparently demarcates the outer reaches of the known world, thereby supplanting the Biblical Gozan River. Secondly, it is portrayed as a river enclosing the Lost Tribes by casting rocks and sand throughout the week, while resting on the seventh day (e.g., *Genesis Rabbah*, p. 73).[2]

The legend of the Sons of Moses (*bnei Moshe*), namely the Levites and Priests that served in the Temple, also turns up in the rabbinic sources. After the first Temple's destruction, so the story goes, a cloud materialized and transported these clerics to a safe haven (*Pesikta Rabbati*, chapter 31). This tale even found its way into Islamic texts. In all likelihood, it is hinted to in the Quran (sura 7 v. 159); and according to some Islamic traditions, Muhammad embarked on his "heavenly voyage" (*miraj*) for the purpose of meeting these same Levites. The story overlapped and at times got intermingled with another Judeo-Muslim legend about a utopian group – the Rechabites. For many years, these traditions existed on a separate basis. However, Eldad's tale merged these snippets – the Ten Tribes, their kings, and the fantastical account of the Sabbath-observant river – into the coherent narrative that is widely known today.

Eldad the Danite visited the Jewish communities along the Mediterranean Basin at a formative moment in their existence. Following Judah's Return to Zion (538 BCE), there were two primary centers of the Jewish world: the Land of Israel and Babylon – populated by the Jews that had chosen not to return. Researchers have shown that the second Temple's destruction (70 CE) did not lead to the complete banishment of Jews from the Land of Israel; and to the best of our knowledge, the same can be said for the Bar Kokhba revolt (132–135 CE). Nevertheless, Jews founded communities throughout the Roman Empire, primarily in Egypt, Asia Minor (present-day Turkey), and Italy. That said, the vast majority of the Jewish people were still concentrated in the two centers: the Land of Israel, under Byzantine rule; and Babylon, under Sasanian rule. These hubs diverged in aspects of their way of thinking as well as their main corpora of literature: the Jerusalem and Babylonian Talmuds.

A wider Jewish geographical dispersion was prompted by the Muslim conquest of the Middle East and the southern and western basins of the Mediterranean Sea. By the time the Umayyads advanced into Provence in 734, the vast majority of the Jewish people found themselves under a single religio-cultural and lingual umbrella – the Arab world – for the first time in centuries. Within this framework, Jews established new communities in, say, North Africa, Andalusia (present-day Spain), and the Caucasus, all of which turned to the classical centers for guidance and support. Consequently, scholars have divided late first-millennium Jewry on the basis of its communities' allegiances to one of the two hubs. The Byzantine and Italian expanses were under the influence of the Land of Israel, whereas North Africa and Spain tied their fate with Babylon. Conversely, both of the centers had affiliated synagogues and institutions in Egypt.

Headed by *geonim* (pl. of *gaon*), large Talmud academies were active in both Babylon and the Land of Israel. Over the course of the ninth century, the Babylonian center shifted to Baghdad – a new city erected by the Abbasids. While also relocating to Baghdad, the academies continued to be referred to by their former places of residence: *Pumpedita* and *Sura*. In addition, the new capital was the seat of the exilarch (*reish galuta*) – an executive, secular office whose hereditary holder presumably led the Jewish world. Though residing in close proximity to the academies, the exilarch was occasionally pitted against their heads. A gaon also presided over the *yeshiva* in Palestine. First located in Jerusalem, the Land of Israel academy moved to Ramla, Tiberias, and finally Tyre, of all places.[3]

Texts discovered in the Cairo Geniza shed light on the complex relations between these two hubs during the Gaonic era, not least their bitter struggles over legal (=Halakhic) methods, authority, and control of the Jewish communities throughout the Diaspora.[4] The past played a decisive role in this "war," as each side presented itself as the custodian of the most genuine tradition. For instance, the Prikoi ben Baboi epistle – a polemical document sent from Babylonian circles to North Africa during the ninth century – claimed that the Land of Israel tradition was impaired by the community's persecution at the hands of the local Christian government. The letter also noted that during the Return to Zion (a millennium before), the House of David's sages and scion remained in Babylon, whereas only commoners went back to Israel. Conversely, the Land of Israel establishment raised the banner of its region's holiness and all that derived from this standing. A case in point was the local ceremony at which the calendar was set for the new Hebrew year on behalf of the entire Jewish world. The jostling between the two centers also had significant economic ramifications. When an affiliated community sent a halakhic inquiry to a gaon, the letter usually included a monetary gift. Likewise, each community constituted a "reservoir" of potential donors to the academy. What is more, this pecuniary dimension explains the chronic struggles between *Sura* and *Pumpedita* and between their respective *geonim* and the exilarch.

This period also bore witness to the emergence and subsequent blossoming of Karaite Jewry, whose founders took issue with the oral law. Although his sway is less than previously assumed, Karaism's ascent is linked to one Anan ben David. Even more than the Rabbinites (i.e. non-Karaites), Karaite Judaism was influenced by Islam. As their name (*bnei mikra* – sons of the Hebrew Bible) suggests, the Karaites placed an emphasis on "the written Torah," and their exegesis of the Bible revolved around a number of interpretive principles. They considered the oral law, above all the Talmud, an extraneous, man-made casuistry. Its criticism of the Rabbinates notwithstanding, the denomination also had traditions that are external to the canon, like their methods for slaughtering meat or performing circumcisions.[5] This, then, is the smoking cauldron of opposing interests that Eldad walked into upon reaching North Africa in the late ninth century.

With this in mind, let us turn our attention to the exchange under review. At the outset of their letter, the community of Kairouan inform R. Zemaḥ that a Jewish traveler claiming to be from the tribe of Dan, Eldad the Danite (*haDani* in Hebrew), has turned up in their city. This mysterious visitor described to them the praxis of the Lost Tribes, their kings, wars, Torah, and language. Summarizing Eldad's account, the community reports that the Tribes live in an ideal society on the edge of the charted world, under the reign of a just monarch. As such, this description constitutes one of the first utopias of the Middle Ages. Only the sons of Moses, in Eldad's telling, are enclosed behind the Sambation River. For their part, the other "lost Jews" are immersed in war with surrounding nations. Though the former always triumph, the fighting endures. As per Eldad's in-depth account of their military service, the enlisted men combine the traits of a warrior and gentleman. The stewards of a "pure" Jewish culture, the Tribes only speak the Holy Tongue. Their Hebrew is indeed mellifluous, but slightly differs from the dialect used by the Kairouanites. For example, it includes some strange words, such as *tintara* for dove, *darmosh* for peppers, etc. In assaying the Danite's Hebrew, the community members displayed the skills of a modern linguist and anthropologist: they pointed to items and asked the sojourner for their words in his unique language; several days later, they repeated the questions in order to make sure that he was consistent. This is the only instance in which the Kairouanites doubted Eldad's story.

The oral tradition that Eldad presented bears a resemblance to that of his hosts, but stands out in a number of ways. To begin with, it reflects a community that had ostensibly been cut off from the rest of the Jewish world since the days of the first Temple. For instance, the Tribes were unaware of the events that are commemorated by the festival of Purim. Eldad unfurled certain elements of the Tribes' Talmud (oral tradition), mainly the laws of kosher slaughtered animals (*ḥulin*). The way Eldad presents it, this tradition was given directly at Mount Sinai and transmitted down to the Tribes' hands by Moses and Joshua and non-other. Nonetheless, there are minor discrepancies between the Eldadian tradition and that of the Kairouanites, which cast doubt on the latter. This dissonance is what motivated the community to reach out to R. Zemaḥ. Eldad's gospel is deemed to be "truer," better, and more "trustworthy" for several reasons. In the first place, it is a "pure tradition." In contrast, the Talmud was "damaged" over the long years of exile under the yoke of the nations. Moreover, the names of sages that inform Mishnaic and Talmudic disputations are absent from the Tribes' code. Instead, they present a direct line of transmission: "Thus we learnt from the mouth of Joshua, from Moses, and from the Almighty."

As such, the subject of the query that the Kairouanites submitted to the gaon is not Eldad's tradition, but rather that of the Rabbinites. In the hope that R. Zemah will clarify the reasons behind these disparities, the community members outline laws of ritual slaughter in Eldad's possession. These laws are formulated in a Biblical language that is archaic even by the standards of the ninth century. For example, they are rife with outdated (Biblical) terms like *tahor* (pure) and *tamei* (defiled), which come at the expense of their widespread Rabbinite parallels: *kasher* (kosher) and *tareif* (ritually unfit). In stressing the differences between these traditions, modern researchers have endeavored to find, *inter alia*, Karaite, Jewish Ethiopian, and Samaritan traces in Eldad's laws.

The Kairouanites' inquiry concludes with the story of the Levites, sons of Moses (discussed below in chapter 3). Following the destruction, the clergy were swept away by a cloud that brought them to a haven along the banks of the Sambation River. Hemmed in on all sides by the waterway, the Levites maintain a utopic and sacred lifestyle. The mighty current of the Sambation upends boulders and sand six days a week, so that the residents are barred from leaving the haven. The flow comes to a standstill on the Sabbath, but the adherence of *bnei Moshe* to the Torah's commandments prevents them from crossing over.

In his response (discussed below in chapter 4), the gaon informs the Kairouanites that news of the Danite has already reached his ears via sages who came across the traveler in what appears to be southern Iraq. R. Zemah then allays their concerns regarding the contradictions between the Eldadian and Rabbinite traditions by reinforcing the latter and playing down the importance of these discrepancies. What is more, he points to the details in the visitor's story that are corroborated by the Midrashic (first centuries) sources at his own disposal. Among the common denominators are the banishment of the Ten Tribes (including that of Dan, well before the first Temple's destruction); the fine attributes of the Israelites; their kings; and the Levites' sanctuary by the mythic river. At this juncture, I would like to allude to the fact that the resemblance between the two accounts stems in part from Eldad's use of identical or very similar sources to assemble his tales.

R. Zemah subsequently proceeds to explain the differences between the traditions. He claims that historical circumstances, foremost among them transmission problems, are responsible for the changes that befell the unwritten tradition from Mount Sinai. However, all of these discrepancies involve minor, technical, and external matters, none of which pertain to core issues. In any event, the gaon repeatedly claims that the tradition in his hands is superior to all others. For the sake of bolstering this argument, he asserts that upon entering the promised land, the Jewish people were preoccupied with conquering the land and thus forgot some of the laws that Joshua ben Nun had taught them. "Doubts" even germinated in Joshua's mind following Moses' demise. Put differently, the traditions, even those in the hand of Joshua, were subjected to some loss over the course of the transmission process.

As noted, R. Zemaḥ ascribes the differences between the two Talmuds to technicalities. He compares these discrepancies to those between the Land of Israel and Babylonian legal codes. In the gaon's estimation, there are several reasons for this state of affairs, none of which pertain to legal content: lingual differences between Babylonian and Land of Israel Aramaic; the fact that the Tribes' gospel was penned in Hebrew; and the schools' disparate approaches to argumentation. Moreover, he argues that the Mishna comprises the Halakha's content, while the Babylonian and Jerusalem Talmuds furnish the explanations and reasons. R. Zemaḥ acknowledges that there are various traditions of the Hebrew Bible's text as well, but most of the discrepancies between them are also of a technical nature touching upon spelling differences, or division of paragraphs.

In all likelihood, the gaon felt as though he was treading on uncertain ground. Above all, he was uncomfortable with the contrived distinction between the written and oral law (Scripture and Talmud). By undermining the conception of "a law given to Moses at Sinai," this measure played into the hands of the Karaites. These concerns appear to be responsible for the admonition in his responsum: "It is unbefitting to interpret every single word, as stated 'It is God's privilege to conceal things' (Proverbs 25:2)."

Besides understating these disparities, R. Zemaḥ raises the possibility that Eldad's transmission was beset by a "profusion of troubles that he underwent and the hardships of the road that torment a man's body." In so doing, he clearly ignores the salient differences between Eldad's laws and those in his Mishna and Talmud. This line of thought only accentuates the rhetorical and ideological character of his answer. For instance, the gaon's claim as to the superiority of his own traditions, namely the Babylonian lore, is predicated on the belief that the tribes of Judah and Benjamin, who comprised the entire populace of the Jewish Community in Babylon, observed the Torah more scrupulously than the Israelites. What is more, he attributes to Eldad a declaration – which our sources are silent about – that the Lost Tribes pray for the welfare of Babylonian sages before that of the rest of the Diaspora. The responsum ends with a reaffirmation of Babylon's ascendant status: not only were the most distinguished scholars and prophets exiled to the banks of the Euphrates River, but they perpetuated an age-old tradition that was passed on directly from the House of David, "from whom the Torah [is disseminated] to the entire [Jewish] people."

Notes

1 At this point, the Kairouanites indeed present a long sampling of the Eldad's laws of slaughtering animals – a topic that will be featured in chapter 5; then comes Eldad's description of the life behind the Sambation River – discussed in chapter 3; R. Zemaḥ's response is summarized below and discussed in chapter 4.

2 Daniel Stein Kokin, "Toward the Source of the *Sambatyon*: Shabbat Discourse and the Origins of the sabbatical River Legend," *AJS Review* 37 (2013): 1–28.

3 For more on the *Geonim*, see: Robert Brody, *The Geonim of Babylonia and the Shaping of Medieval Jewish Culture* (Yale 1998).

4 On the Geniza: Adina Hoffman and Peter Cole, *Sacred Trash: The Lost and Found World of the Cairo Geniza* (New York 2011).

5 On the Karaites: Meira Polliack (ed.), *Karaite Judaism: A Guide to its History and Literary Sources* (Leiden – Boston 2003).

2 Truth and false

Ḥasdai ibn Shaprut's letter to Joseph King of Khazar (Al-Andalus, 10th century):

> In the days of our forefathers, a sagacious man of Israel turned up in our community. He would display his lineage in the tribe of Dan as far back as Dan the son of Jacob. He would fluently speak [Hebrew] and had a word for everything in the Holy Tongue. What is more nothing escaped his eye. Upon getting ready to preach, he would say ... "Othniel ben Knaz received from Joshua from Moses and from the Almighty."

R. Moshe of Narbonne's description of the land of the Ten Lost Tribes (11th century):

> Among them there is no impure animal, domesticated or wild, and no impure fowl and no type of ground crawler. And with them is sheep and cattle.

To date, not a single researcher has outright denied the existence of Eldad the Danite. However, the scholarship is divided over the following questions: Was Eldad a charlatan? Was he a Karaite, a Rabbinite, or a Samaritan? And did he come from Ethiopia, Yemen, or perhaps China? Is the Danite's lore real or a fabrication? What is his Talmud's relation to the Rabbinic literature? Did this adventurer manage to pull the wool over the eyes of Jews the world-over from the ninth century onwards? Or was he merely "a publically-adored story teller"[1] who, as accepted in this vocation, "fused truth and fiction" in his works?[2] These are indeed the sort of topics that positivist historians contend with, and the road to answering these questions runs through a solution to the philological stumbling block that Eldad's writings place before scholars. Hence the current chapter's principal research method is philological – the main tool of positivist historians. In other words, our objective is, first, to reconstruct the original wording of the texts under review.[3]

The primary full and coherent sources – albeit not necessarily the most authentic ones – that pertain to Eldad are fifteenth-century prints of *Sefer Eldad* (The Book of Eldad) and *Shalshelet ha-kabbalah* (The Chain of the Tradition) by Gedalyah ibn Yahya.[4] A host of other texts that are ascribed to Eldad were commonplace among medieval Jews: in legal writings, stories, midrash, polemical literature, and grammar. Modern researchers have added to this list every text containing the phrase "Our rabbi Joshua said in the name of Moses in the name of the Almighty," or merely "Joshua ben Nun said." Until the nascent stages of the print era, this corpus encompassed twenty manuscripts and over thirty citations and references in an assortment of languages and genres. This panoply of texts warrants the heading "the Eldad literature." Out of all these documents, however, which ones were actually penned by Eldad or another writer in that same ninth-century environment? With respect to the present chapter, was the query to Zemah ben Hayim and his responsum (discussed in chapter 4) authentic or not?

To begin with, we will survey the annals of the pertinent research. Eldad's riveting corpus attracted many scholars, who indeed compiled and sorted the material. The first major milestone in this far-reaching enterprise is the contribution of Abraham Epstein (1841–1918), who collected and juxtaposed the sundry versions of the Danite's writing in a book that came out in 1891.[5] All told, he published sixteen of these texts, which he divided into four versions of halakhic output and twelve versions of stories, along with three additional short references to the laws and eight to the tales.[6] Epstein averred that Eldad represents a genuine Jewish community. Equivocating over its precise location, he averred that this community was somewhere in Yemen or south-eastern Africa; owing to the resemblance the scholar detected between Eldad's customs and those of Ethiopian Jewry, he was most likely from the vicinity of Ethiopia. Epstein reached this conclusion on the basis of several findings: Eldad's knowledge of Arabic (as opposed to the Kairouanites' report); and given the differences between Eldad's gospel and the Babylonian Talmud, he came from a region in which the latter was unknown. Epstein pointed to the similarities between the Danite's laws of slaughter of animals and the laws of slaughtering sacrifices in the Temple. For instance, in the said researcher's view, some of the odd traditions in Eldad's "Talmud" were predicated on the requirement that all blood be meticulously removed from sacrificed animals. This discovery also tipped the scales in favor of the view that Eldad was representative of an "authentic" community, or at least an ancient one. Furthermore, these laws suggest that he was from Ethiopia or further south (see the final chapter below). Replete with insightful comments, Epstein's edition of *Sefer Eldad* underpins the scholarship on this figure and his writings.

A year after the release of Epstein's book, David Heinrich Müller (1842–1911) published a study aimed at clarifying the relation between the different versions of these stories.[7] Drawing on two first prints and six manuscripts, he put out Zemaḥ b. Ḥayim's above-noted responsum (save for the halakhic section), a letter to the communities of Spain attributed to Eldad, parts of Eldad's midrash on the sons of Moses, and his descriptions of the Ten Tribes. In addition to outlining the genealogy ("family tree") of the principal versions, Müller synopsized the above-mentioned texts in table form. By virtue of his research on Eldad and, all the more so, his expertise on the Arabian Peninsula, particularly Yemen, the scholar posited that Eldad was a native of southern Arabia.

In 1908, Max Schloessinger (1877–1944) unveiled two fragments from the recently-discovered Cairo Geniza. Due to their eleventh-century provenance, these documents are highly credible sources. On the basis of these findings, Schloessinger put out a critical edition of Eldad's laws (halakha),[8] which is brimming with halakhic, linguistic, and even zoological explanations. That said, the reconstructed text is eclectic, for Schloessinger merged together eleven different texts (manuscripts, prints, Geniza fragments, and shards of quotations) using the "cut and paste (then: scissors-and-glue)" method.

The theory as to Eldad's Yemenite origins was bolstered by Shelomo Morag's efforts to determine the adventurer's origins by dint of the Hebrew on his lips.[9] The linguist opined that there are clear vestiges of Arabic and Syriac in Eldad's language. In Morag's estimation, the only ninth-century Jewish community where such a lingual reality was feasible is Najran – a town in north Yemen. A similar linguistic study on the part of Yitzchak Gluska also concluded that Eldad was from north Yemen, but not necessarily Najran.[10]

Much to our regret, the findings of these two scholars lack a solid philological basis. The cardinal flaw in Morag's research is his over-reliance on the Schloessinger edition. More specifically, he treated the eclectic version that Schloessinger had intermingled from variance sources as a single text. Gluska partially avoided this problem by using a single version (from the *shechita* laws of Shmuel ibn Jama'a, which are discussed below). However, the scholar did not check the work's manuscript editions for revisions – a step that also would have enabled him to see the evolution of the Danite's texts. The point of departure of both these studies is that Eldad was from Ethiopia or the Arabian Peninsula. Since neither linguist found remnants of Ge'ez or Ethiopic, they both settled on Arabia as the place of origin. However, this hypothesis ignores the earlier studies that left open the possibility of, say, China and Persia.[11]

History is not the study of the past, but the study of remnants that have been left to us from the past. Solving the riddle of Eldad the person rests, first and foremost, on the discipline of philology – on our capacity to reconstruct the texts that are ascribed to him, to distinguish what he personally wrote from erroneous attributions, and to identify those texts that have nothing to do with this figure. The key to this riddle lies in the Kairouan Jewish community's epistle[12] to Zemaḥ gaon and his responsum. In their query, the Kairouanites recount the story of Eldad the Danite. In addition, they refer to the unique Hebrew on his tongue and offer a synopsis of his laws. Drawing on this exchange, scholars have attributed other texts to Eldad, above all *midrashim* and legal traditions in which his name is not expressly noted. Whereas the putative author of these texts lived in the ninth century, the earliest unabridged version of the responsum (the question and the answer) that survives can be found in an incunabulum of *Sefer Eldad ha-Dani* that was put out by Abraham Conat in 1480.[13] Conat is known to have embarked on a quest for pertinent manuscripts in Turkey and other destinations, but we are completely in the dark as to the actual sources that were at his disposal.[14] Although this incunabulum came out some 500 years after the presumed original, its veracity is substantiated by a fragment from the Geniza that Schloessinger dated to no later than the 1200s.[15] While attesting to the existence of such a text in the East during an erstwhile period, the fragment also indicates that the wording was different. Its late provenance notwithstanding, Conat's version indeed undergirds the discussion on Eldad's writings, to the point where the hands of scholars would be tied without this print.

All the components of the Eldad literature are accounted for in the letter from Kirouan, which was spurred on by their bewilderment over the differences between the Danite's gospel and the Mishna and Talmud, as well as his strange line of transmission: "Their lore ... makes no mention of any sage, either from the Mishna or the Talmud; instead, every halakha opens with the following words: 'Thus we learnt from the mouth of Joshua, from Moses, and from the Almighty.'" This passage is followed by the linchpin of the Eldad corpus: a brief "summary" of his laws of *shechita*. Another important element of this body of works is the stories, which can be divided into three categories. The first is Eldad's personal experiences. The second is the history of the Ten Tribes: Dan's exile before the Temple's destruction; and information concerning the sons of Moses, not least their enclosure beyond the Sambation River. Last but not least are accounts of the Ten Tribes during Eldad's own lifetime: their location, norms, wars, language, and traditions. Facets of the Danite's speech constitute an auxiliary branch of this literature. In its query, the Kairouan Jewish community depicts the visitor's unusual language: "He calls a dove a '*tintara*,' a bird a '*requt*,' and pepper a '*darmosh*.'" Furthermore, the letter notes that Hebrew is the only language he speaks.

This corpus steadily expanded over the generations, be it through the attribution of more works to Eldad, the augmentation of existing texts, and the discovery of additional works by the author. To begin with, there are different versions of Eldad's laws: fragments from the Geniza; less truncated versions than the above-cited "summary" of the Kairouanites' missive, and citations in the halakhic literature. Moreover, details were added to a handful of the stories. For instance, a version of a letter by Eldad expounds on the author's journey from his place of origin to North Africa and beyond. Among its innovations is a nasty encounter with cannibals, miraculous escape, and a depiction of the Ten Tribes' far-flung lands – stories that Adam Silverstein compares to the Sinbad literature.[16] In a similar fashion, different versions of these accounts of the Tribes, especially the exile of Dan, the annals of *bnei Moshe*, and descriptions of the Sambation River, surface within the framework of the Midrashic literature. Furthermore, medieval grammars comment on the sojourner's unique dialect of Hebrew and knowledge thereof; and exegetes subsequently cited these testimonies. As noted, some of these elaborations do not mention Eldad's name.[17] However, scholars have ascribed these works to him on the basis of their resemblance to the Kairouanites' exchange with R. Zemaḥ or, all the more so, the use of the above-noted catchphrase: "Our rabbi Joshua said in the name of Moses in the name of the Almighty," or the truncated "Joshua said."

In sum, the lone channel through which Eldad's texts have survived is copies that were rendered hundreds of years after his passing. It is only natural, then, that there are doubts as to whether some of these works should be attributed to him. Drawing on positivist historical methods, we will search for apocryphal or corresponding evidence of Eldad's existence. In fact, early testimonies indicate that this figure indeed walked the Earth. There is evidence, say, of a personal meeting with Judah ibn Kuraish (a late ninth-century grammarian in North Africa), during which the sojourner defined the word root "shin-gimel-hei" as *'esek* ("stake" or "interest" in Modern Hebrew). While this encounter goes unmentioned in ibn Kuraish's book, Jonah ibn Janah (an early eleventh-century grammarian in southern Spain) refers to it in his own disquisition of this word: "And a few of the commentators already spoke of this, including Judah ibn Kuraish who said that he heard the Danite man say I have a *shguya* in this matter, I have an *'esek.*"[18] Incidentally, this word does not turn up in the surviving Eldadian corpus. At any rate, these sources bear witness to the fact that the traveler's definitions were accepted by virtue of his expertise in the Hebrew language and correct usage. Moreover, his very utterances were perceived as exemplars of lingual propriety. This authority stems from the fact that Eldad was indeed considered a "Danite," namely the keeper of ethnic and lingual traditions that stem directly from Mt. Sinai.

Further testimony as to Eldad's existence surfaces in a letter by Ḥasdai ibn Shaprut, the famed Jewish Andalusian vizier, to King Joseph of Khazar. In this letter he describes a man of the tribe of Dan turning up in "our community." This Danite "would fluently speak [Hebrew] and had a word for everything in the holy tongue ... upon getting ready to preach, he would say: 'Othniel ben Knaz received from Joshua from Moses and from the Almighty.'"[19]

It stands to reason that there was but one "Danite" wandering through North Africa (and perhaps even Spain) in the centuries before the lifetimes of Ḥasdai ibn Shaprut and ibn Kuraish.[20] The Jewish vizier indeed mentions three pillars of the Eldad literature: his Danite lineage (in the stories), the fluency of his Hebrew (in works of grammar), and his unique set of laws. Unlike the Kairouanites' missive, it is within the realm of the possible that Eldad himself did not reach Spain. We do not necessarily have to take Hasdai's statement "In the days of our forefathers, a sagacious man of Israel turned up in **our** community" at face value. More specifically, the vizier's use of the word "our" could refer to Kairouan, especially given the fact that the letter was sent to addressees beyond the dark mountains who would not necessarily distinguish between Spain and North Africa. Continuing to the early eleventh century, Jews at Kairouan already possessed an "Eldad literature" whose branches overlap with the extant corpus. A case in point in the response of Nissim ben Jacob (990–1057) to the question of whether the Ten Tribes exist: "The story of the Danite, his epistle, and the [laws for] slaughtering meat that he transmitted, as well as the [Hebrew] words that were recalled from him are all real proof of this."[21] As documented in two prominent medieval sources, there was a *Sefer Eldad ha-Dani* (Book of Eldad the Danite) – one consisting of, at the very least, his personal story including the fantastical journeys, and traditions on the Ten Tribes and the sons of Moses – from as early as the twelfth century, both in the East and West.[22]

Even if all the works in this corpus cannot be attributed to Eldad, one can assume, with a fair degree of certainty, that the person existed. In all likelihood, he indeed claimed to be from the Ten Tribes and carried in his satchel laws of *shechita* and unique lingual traditions. However, we have yet to resolve the following matters: Is Eldad's story true? Was he indeed from the land of the Danites? Here, the discipline of philology might be of service.

Perusing the transmission of the sources that are connected to Eldad has brought us one step closer to answering the question of whether or not he was telling the truth. Let us now examine some of these sources. Abraham Epstein provides a number of Eldad's tales that "were absorbed" into a midrash of R. Moshe ha-Darshan (the Preacher). The head of Narbonne's yeshiva during the first half of the eleventh century, R. Moshe preserved forgotten traditions. Among these were ancient traditions from the Qumran literature, the apocrypha, and lost midrashes. The latter apparently derived from the Land of Israel, but were transmitted through Byzantium and eventually found their way to south France. While most of his own writings are no longer extant, some have been preserved in later citations.[23] With respect to the topic at hand, Moshe ha-Darshan brought a midrash on the Ten Tribes that runs parallel to Eldad's stories. Although the name Eldad does not appear in this midrash, Epstein identified it with the Danite on the basis of the introductory phrase: "Joshua ben Nun said in the name of Moses, may peace be upon him, in the name of the Almighty." This hypothesis is bolstered by a number of other characteristic turns of phrase.[24] That said, are these similarities enough to definitively attribute this version to the Danite?

As noted, Zemaḥ ben Ḥayim already pointed to the fact that Eldad's reports of the sons of Moses and the Sambation River have ancient sources.[25] In my estimation, Moshe ha-Darshan's version is of utmost importance to understanding the evolution of the corpus at hand. The Provençal Rabbi's work was the shortest version of all these sorts of accounts. Scholars tended to view the Eldadian parallels in this midrash as a précis of another incarnation of this tale. However, the argument can be made that the stories are independent and that they reached Moshe ha-Darshan via another outlet. In this case they predate Eldad and they might represent such antecedent materials Eldad used to spin his own tale.[26]

A comparison of Moshe ha-Darshan's version to the others, which are appreciably longer, demonstrates that they are an elaboration of the former. Put differently, ha-Darshan's rendering is not a summary of the others, but their origin. The latter fill in minute details of general story lines in the earlier version. To wit, they expound on the wars of the Ten Tribes; a case in point is a speech given to equestrians heading out for battle. Whereas Moshe ha-Darshan merely touches on the Israelites' homes, animals, and nutrition, the rest of the versions describe these houses and enumerate the types of animals and agricultural products in the members' possession. For example,

Moshe ha-Darshan's Midrash (Bereisheet Rabbati)	Eldad the Danite (MS London, the British Library 27129)
Among them there is no impure animal, domesticated or wild, and no impure fowl and no type of ground crawler	And there is not with them something defiled, an impure fowl, an impure domesticated animal, or an impure wild animal, and no flies, fleas, wild beasts [i.e., predators], snakes, and scorpions, and no wolves, dogs, foxes, lion cubs, and tigers; and even lice they do not have;
And with them is sheep and cattle	instead, [all they possess is] sheep and cattle

Aside for animals and foods, the other versions list the names of the neighboring kings, judges, and nations. For instance, "And the name of their king is Uziel ben Malkiel Yakuli from the sons of Oholiab; and sitting in judgement over them is Abdan ben Meshiel from the tribe of Asher." Among the nations that come up in these texts are "Arva, Tiska, Kamsua, Tiva, Karma, and Kakua."[27] While Moshe ha-Darshan asserts that the members of the Ten Tribes do not lie under oath, some of the versions add a warning to those who might commit such an offense: their children are liable to die prematurely; other versions state that among the tribes whoever lies – at all – dies immediately.[28] These examples suffice to demonstrate that at the outset, there was a short version of this midrash. In the ensuing centuries, the story was plumped up with more information, courtesy of the fertile imagination of one or more writers. Whether this was Eldad or others is impossible to determine.

Another unique aspect of Moshe ha-Darshan's midrash is that it makes no mention of Eldad the Danite. In contrast, the other versions have what can be dubbed an "Eldadian stratum": narrated in the first person, this layer consists of the story of the protagonist's journey and a brief description of the Tribes' lore as well as the story of the sons of Moses. For the purpose of explaining how this latter information fell into the globetrotter's hands, the Eldadian stratum includes a description of the ties between the sons of Moses and the rest of the tribes.

What is more, the crux of a handful of these additions and elaborations – Judge Abdun, King Addiel, and the description of the Tribes' wars and "battle cry," *inter alia* – can be found in the Kairouan letter to Zemaḥ gaon (but not in Moshe ha-Darshan's version). It is these same elements that connect several of these texts to the Danite.

Given the surfeit of details involved, let us recap the findings to this point. First, Moshe ha-Darshan's version antecedes all the others. Second, the material pertaining to Eldad that was added to the original, such as the Tribes' lore, and the elaboration of topics that were raised in the Kairouanites' letter comprises the Eldadian strata. If so, R. Moshe's legends on sons of Moses and the Ten Tribes are independent of and most likely predated Eldad. This succession attests to the existence, at a certain stage, of similar or parallel texts to those of Eldad. Against this backdrop, it is hardly a quantum leap to reach the conclusion that he did not create these myths. Instead, Eldad (or someone that attributed these tales to him) made use of preexisting texts, like Moshe ha-Darshan's midrash, which the former adapted to suit his own needs. This material naturally postdates the second Temple (and certainly the first Temple, to which the Danite referred). Consequently, it is obvious that Eldad was not a member of the Ten Tribes, and was a member (though distant) of the post-Temple, even Rabbinic, Jewish world. For the sake of avoiding another longwinded philological discussion, we will suffice with saying that this hypothesis is corroborated by the findings from Eldad's legal texts (halakha).[29]

Our philological investigation has turned the heretofore accepted chronology of texts on its head, and advanced our understanding of the "origins" of Eldad. Nevertheless, we have still not managed to draw a clear line between fact and fiction in the history of this corpus. Even after all that has been revealed – Eldad apparently existed, but his stories and laws, regardless of whether they were the fruit of his own labor or merely attributed to him, are based on earlier sources – one can still plausibly advocate, two antithetical points of departure: 1. Eldad represents a specific, actual community, and his story reflects the self-perception of this group, namely that its members derive from the Ten Tribes (hence his story is "true"). 2. There was indeed a person by the name of Eldad the Danite, but the eponymous literature is the product of subsequent generations that "pinned" these works on him (hence "false"). This irresolution is emblematic of contemporary methodological difficulties in all that concerns establishing the historical truth. These challenges intersect with modern questions as to what is an "author" of a medieval text and how should we understand the veracity of such texts.[30] Put differently, even after conducting a historical and philological study that has substantially reduced the number of possible scenarios, we are still left with a pair of dichotomous options: true or false.

Notes

1 Menahem Ben-Sasson, *Emergence of the Local Jewish Community in the Muslim World, Qayrawan, 800-1057* (Jerusalem 1996) [henceforth: Ben-Sasson], 274 [Hebrew].

2 Abraham Epstein, *Kitvei R. Avraham Epstein*, ed. Abraham Meir Habermann, vol. I (Jerusalem 1950), 24 [Hebrew].

3 James Turner, *Philology: The Forgotten Origins of the Modern Humanities* (Princeton 2014).

4 *Sefer Eldad ha-Dani*, first print (Mantua 1480); Gedalyah ibn Yaḥya, *Shalshelet ha-kabbalah* (Venice 1587), 37b.

5 Abraham Epstein, *Sefer Eldad ha-Dani* (Vienna 1891). Reprinted with additions, appendixes, notes, and other versions: idem, *Kitvei R. Avraham Epstein* [henceforth: Epstein].

6 In the revised Epstein edition, Habermann added another four stories – all of them from the books of Müller and Schloessinger (discussed below) – as well as a list of Eldad's prints consisting of 53 items.

7 David Heinrich Müller, *Die Recensionen und Versionen des Eldad had-Dânî* (Vienna 1892) [henceforth: Müller].

8 Max Schloessinger, *The Ritual of Eldad ha-Dani* (Leipzig and New York 1908) [henceforth: Schloessinger]. Krauss' opinion that Eldad came from central Asia is also worth mentioning: Samuel Krauss, "New Light on Geographical Information of Eldad Hadani and Benjamin of Tudela," *Tarbiẓ* 8 (1936), 225–228 [Hebrew].

9 Shlomo Morag, "Eldad Haddani's Hebrew and the Problem of his Provenance," *Tarbiẓ* 66 (1997): 223–246 [Hebrew].

10 Yitzchak Gluska, "Eldad the Danite of Yemen and the Language of His Writing," in Aharaon Gaimani et al., eds., *Sons of Yemen: Studies on Yemenite Jewry and its Heritage* (Ramat Gan 2011), 137–268 [Hebrew].

11 David J. Wasserstein takes stock of this literature in idem, "Eldad ha-Dani and Prester John," in Charles F. Beckingham and Bernard Hamilton, eds., *Prester John, the Mongols and the Ten Lost Tribes* (Aldershot, UK and Brookfield, VT 1996), 213–236 [henceforth: Wasserstein].

12 For a comprehensive look at the Kairouan community during this period, see Ben-Sasson.

13 A different, more succinct version turns up in Gedalyah ibn Yaḥya, *Shalshelet ha-kabbalah*, 37b.

14 Abraham Conat and his sources are discussed in V. Colorni, "Abraham Conat, primo stampatore di opere ebraiche in Mantova e la cronologia delle sue edizioni," *La Bibliofilía* 83/2 (1981): 113–128.

15 Schloessinger, 116–117.

16 Adam Silverstein, "From Markets to Marvels: Jews on the Maritime Route to China ca. 850-ca. 950 CE," *Journal of Jewish Studies* 58/1 (Spring 2007): 91–104.

17 What is more, some of these texts are attributed to different figures, such as "Elchanan the Merchant" in *Sefer ha-zikhronot* (The Book of Memoirs), or *Hilchot Eretz Yisrael*, and other works from the *tosafot* literature (medieval commentaries on the Talmud).

20   *Truth and false*

18 Abu al-Walīd Marwān ibn Ganaḥ, *Sefer ha-Shorashim, Wurzelwörterbuch der Hebräischen Sprache, von Abulwalîd Merwân ibn Gânāḥ*, W. Bacher (ed.) (Berlin 1896), 497; Epstein, 101.
19 Павел К. Кёкёвцёв, *Еврейскё-хазарская переписка в X веке* (=Pavel K. Kokovtsov, *Hebrew-Khazarian Correspondence of the Xth Century*) (Leningrad 1932), 11–12; Epstein, 100. The context behind this particular passage is Hasdai's interest in whether, like Eldad, the Khazars only speak Hebrew.
20 It could very well be that there were other "Danites" inhabiting the known medieval Jewish world. Ibn Kuraish recounts the words of "the Danite sons who came to us from the Land of Israel" (Epstein, 102). Furthermore, a martyr of the Rhineland Massacres of 1096, Master Judah ben Abraham, was reportedly "from the Danite tribe." See *Hebräische Berichte über die Judenverfolgungen während des Ersten Kreuzzugs*, Eva Haverkamp (Hg.) (Hannover 2005), 431. Jeremy Cohen discusses this martyr in idem, *Sanctifying the Name of God: Jewish Memories of the First Crusade* (Philadelphia 2004), 154–157.
21 Abraham Poznański, "Compilations from *Sefer megilat starim* by Our Rabbi Nissim ben R. Jacob of Kairouan," *Ha-tzofeh le-ḥokhmat Yisrael*, vol. vii (1923), # 28, 22–23 [Hebrew]; Ben-Sasson, 154–157.
22 Judah Hadassi, *Eshkol ha-kofer* (Gözleve [Yevpatoria] 1836), # 60–61, 29b; Abraham Ibn Ezra, *Commentary on Exodus*, 2:22 [both in Hebrew]. According to this scholar, one should not believe "what is written in … *the book of Eldad*."
23 For an in-depth look at R. Moshe ha-darshan, see Hannanel Mack, *The Mystery of Rabbi Moshe Hadarshan* (Jerusalem 2010) [Hebrew]. For an abridged version of the text at hand, see Epstein 64–67; also see the discussion in ibid., 24–25.
24 Epstein, 5, 104, ns. 4 and 8; 107, n. 10.
25 See the sources that are cited in Epstein, 45–46, n. 12.
26 Neubauer weighed this sort of argument, but abandoned it. Adolf Neubauer, "Where are the Ten Lost Tribes, II – Eldad the Danite," *JQR* 1 (1889): 114.
27 This is taken from the same manuscript that came up in the previous example. All of them appear in Müller, 59, 63.
28 In all likelihood, this warning alludes to the Babylonian Talmud, Shabbat, 32b: "Owing to the iniquity of oaths, children will die when they are small."
29 For other references to sons of Moses living "beyond the wilderness," see Aaron Z. Aescoly, *Jewish Messianic Movements* (Jerusalem 1987), 154 [Hebrew]; Adolf Neubauer, "Sources relating the Ten Tribes and the Sons of Moses," *Kobez al Jad* IV (1888): 9 [Hebrew]; Epstein, 45–46, n. 12; M. Seligsohn, "Sambation," *Jewish Encyclopedia* (1906), 682b–683a. In all likelihood, these stories anteceded the birth of Eldad the Danite. We will return to Eldad's legal writings in chapter 5.
30 These questions are accented, for example, in Jean-Claude Schmitt, *The Conversion of Herman the Jew: Autobiography, History and Fiction in the Twelfth Century*, tr. Alex J. Novikoff (Philadelphia 2010).

3 Myth and reality

The continuation of Kairouan's query to R. Zemaḥ gaon:

What is more, he [i.e. Eldad] told us that when the Temple was destroyed, the Jews were exiled to Babylon, the Chaldeans stood over the sons of Moses [i.e., the Levites who used to sing in the Temple] and ordered them to sing one of the songs of Zion. The sons of Moses stood and wailed before the Holy One blessed be He, and cut their fingers with their teeth, saying: "These are the fingers with which we played [musical instruments] in the Temple. How are we to play with them in an impure land?" A cloud then came and carried them, along with their tents and their sheep and cattle, to Evilas and dropped them off there during the night. Moreover, Eldad told us that "Our fathers, who heard from their fathers, told us that that same night they heard a great noise; and in the morning, they saw legions of mighty Levites. [God] had enclosed them by a river that upended rocks and sand in a place where there had never previously been a river." To this day, the river clamorously flings rocks and stones without water. If the river were to hit a mountain of iron, the latter would be shattered. All six days of the week, the river upends stones and sand without a drop of water; and on the Sabbath it rests. At the twilight hour of Friday, a cloud descends, and no one can approach the river until Saturday night. Its name is the *Sambation*, and we call it *Sabatino*. There are places where the river is no wider than sixty cubits; and we and the Levites stand on opposite sides of the river and converse with each other. They are hemmed in because the river surrounds them; we are unable to join them, and they are unable to leave. In their midst, there is not a single wild beast, an impure domesticated animal, abominable creatures, or insects; everyone has sheep and cattle, and they plow and sow [their fields]. [The Jews on either side of the river] ask each other questions. And [the Levites] told them of the Temple's destruction, of which the Danites had no inkling. At any rate, following the destruction of the Temple, Naphtali, Gad, and Asher came to Dan [who left the land of Israel before the destruction]. At the outset, they [i.e., the three tribes] resided with Issachar, in their cities. However, they would quarrel with them [i.e., with Issachar], as the latter would say "You are the descendants of handmaidens." Fearing that a war would breakout between them, they left and journeyed until reaching Dan and the four tribes settled in one place.

In the previous chapter, we determined that Eldad (or other authors in his name) drew on ancient material to construct his legends. This allows us to take stock of the differences between Danite's stories and both earlier works and later adaptations of his own yield. More specifically, we will examine the image that he projects onto the Ten Tribes, how this narrative represents his time and place, and its later impact on Jewish culture. To this end, a comparative literary analysis will be conducted forthwith on descriptions of the Lost Tribes.

Building on the early, skeletal texts, exampled by R. Moshe ha-Darshan's midrash, writers added various details, like the names of kings, the army's rotational conscription, and the animals that the Israelites kept. The goal of this was to improve on the verisimilitude of the original so that it would ring true. As noted earlier, this information is part of "the Eldadian stratum." Besides the globetrotter's personal story, it provides complementary details, like references to the Tribes' lore, their rules of *shechita*, and the connection between the Danites and the sons of Moses. This is presented as a professed firsthand, eye-witness account. I see no way of determining whether it was Eldad himself or later generations that integrated the ancient legends into the eponymous tradition. Regardless of the authorship, the crux of the matter is the impressive result of this undertaking: an anonymous midrash was transformed into a personal testimony that constitutes the very first work of fictional-cum-autobiographical travel literature produced in the Hebrew language.

More specifically, this elaboration involved the personalization of general knowledge – its juxtaposition and anchoring to a historical figure. Insofar as the author(s) was concerned, the benefits from this step are twofold. First, it transformed anonymous knowledge into personal testimony via a transmission process that bolstered its credibility. Second, this endeavor rendered abstract knowledge concrete, thereby giving it a presence in the everyday life of the Jewish masses.[1]

What, then, was the impetus behind this enterprise? Silverstein points to the influence of literary genres in the Muslim expanse – travel, adventure, and "rescue" literature (such as Sinbad) – that, like the Eldad stories, were often written in the first-person.[2] Another explanation accentuates the social context. Admiel Kosman hones in on a legend concerning the names that Adam, the first human, gives to creatures in the Garden of Eden that has a version in the Eldad literature.[3] While this legend is beyond the scope of the present book, Kosman's insights are relevant to the topic at hand. This story, the scholar writes, suited the ideological needs of the embryonic Jewish Diaspora at the outset of the Middle Ages. His analysis shows that this story identifies Adam with the Jewish people, whereas the figure of Satan, who confronts the first human, represents the nations of the world. God helps the meek Jew, by imbuing him with divine wisdom and other tools (i.e., cunning) to defeat Satan. In addition, the Lord promises Adam eternal life (i.e., redemption from the Exile). The implicit message of this legend is that in lieu of political power, the Jewish people can count on Providence and their own wiles to survive the travails of the Diaspora.

Yet another explanation centers around the specific field of knowledge under review –information as to the survival of the Ten Tribes. It could very well be that someone took issue with the earlier outlooks and demanded evidence as to the veracity of the accounts on the Israelites, such as a letter by Prester John (discussed in chapter 4). In the absence of any knowledge of such reservations, though, we must abandon this direction. Instead, the focus will shift to the consensus view: due to the travails of the Exile, the scattering of the Jews, the lack of a national horizon, and the fact that Judaism had become a "despised religion" (as Yehuda ha-Levi put it) among the nations, there was a heightened need to reaffirm prior information concerning the whereabouts of the Lost Tribes. Not only was it imperative to confirm this age-old myth, but to use this story and actualize it for the sake of lifting the flagging spirits of the Diaspora communities. Eldad (the real or imagined figure) was the right man in the right place. The news Eldad brought about the Tribes had a highly psychological impact. To begin with, these stories gave the Jews the sense that they were allied with a force – the mythical Ten Tribes, kings, and warriors included – that far exceeded their own worldly power. Second, as Abraham Gross remarked, these myths filled a theological role in the Jewish–Christian polemic.[4] Based on Genesis 40:10 ("the scepter shall not depart from Judah, nor a lawgiver from between his feet, until Shiloh come"), the Christians argued that the utter lack of Jewish sovereignty – the scepter of Judah has departed – is evidence that Shiloh [i.e., Jesus] has arrived.

In response, the Jews pointed to some remnants of political power, such as the *rashai galuta* (exilarchs) in Babylon.[5] With the reintegration of the Eldad corpus into Jewish life, the rabbis at the forefront of this polemic could also raise the banner of the autonomous Israelites.[6]

Nevertheless, a comparison between the many descriptions of the Lost Tribes shows that Eldad's version stands out from the rest. The Tribes are already mentioned in the Talmudic and Midrashic literature, which located them beyond the Sambation River. While some of the early texts do ascribe magical properties to this waterway,[7] the later sources went so far as to portray the entire land of the Ten Tribes as a wondrous utopia in which gold flows in the rivers and all the inhabitants live forever.[8] Eldad's portrayal, though, is devoid of these elements. He relegates the miraculous, fantastical, and utopic to the sons of Moses, who are the only Israelites enclosed behind the Sambation River. The rest of these Jews maintain rather ordinary, unmagical lifestyles. What is more, the argument can be made that they fail to live up to their own mythical image. The lion's share of Eldad's account is devoted to the army's operations along the border. The Tribes' intrepid equestrian warriors frighten off the enemy with their battle cry. God-fearing Jews, they refrain from fighting on Shabbat unless attacked; the spoils of war are shared with Torah scholars; and their king (named Adiel in some of the versions) is an exemplary leader. If the Israelites are indeed such tenacious warriors, why have they yet to drive their foes beyond the dark mountains, secure the peace, and return to their homestead until the end of their days? It seems as though the answer to this question lies in the precise moment at which the Danite arrived on the scene and in his target audience. Drawing on Kosman's insights, Eldad's emergence coincided with the inception of the Jewish Diaspora (which steadily coalesced in the aftermath of the Muslim conquest) and the recognition that for years to come, the Jews would constitute an ethnic minority, devoid of sovereignty, political power, or an army, and beholden to a ruling Muslim or Christian society.

The descriptions of the Ten Tribes, particularly in the Eldad literature, germinated a seed of hope in Jewish society that it would once again become a normal, independent player on the world stage. For this very reason, the Danite eschews portraying the Tribes as wondrous thaumaturges. On the contrary, he situates them in a realistic political setting and in a quotidian light. They are warriors sitting on their land, under the dominion of a monarch presiding over a just and worthy government. The wide circulation of the Eldad corpus throughout the Middle Ages, both in the East and West, attests to the fact that these stories helped Diaspora Jewry contend with enduring frailties: the sense of detachment; the lack of a true government or military power; and political and religious inferiority.

There is one last significant difference between Eldad's account and the earlier and later ones. Not only did the Danite return the Ten Tribes to the spotlight of Jewish, as well as Muslim and Christian, culture after ages in the shadows, but he extricated them from their prison behind the raging Sambation River. In his telling, only the sons of Moses remain hemmed in by the mythical waterway, while the other tribes are scattered along the borders of the known world. By linking these stories with current events and making them more accessible to a wider audience, Eldad infused them with more than a whiff of messianism. In essence, he was saying that the Tribes are just around the corner, waiting in the wings and keeping a watchful eye on the plight of their brethren. As we will see, this outlook carried the hint of a threat against the Christian and Muslim powers that be. The later revisions of these myths, however, could not sustain these motifs. On the one hand, a bevy of fantastical details were added to these stories; on the other hand, all the Ten Tribes were once again closed off behind the banks of the Sambation River, where they would remain until the Lord decided to emancipate his people from the shackles of the exile. Over the long haul, then, the apocalyptic notion that the Tribes were within arm's reach was too much to bear.

Paling in comparison to the wondrous accounts of distant utopian lands, which typically inform other descriptions of the Lost Tribes that were commonplace during the Middle Ages and remain so to this day, Eldad's protagonists maintain a normal, practically mundane life. This banality was indeed the secret behind these legends' allure, being that the quotidian, realistic, political, free existence of the Jews at the inception of the Diaspora was indeed a desired myth.

Notes

1 See Abraham Gross, "The Ten Tribes and the Kingdom of Prester John – Rumors and Investigations before and after the Expulsion from Spain," *Pe'amim* 48 (1991): 5–41, esp. 8 [Hebrew].
2 Silverstein, "From Markets to Marvels," 91–104.
3 Admiel Kosman, "The Aggadah about the Conflict between Adam and the Angels over the Naming of the Animals according to the Eldad ha-Dani Version," *Mo'ed* 13 (2003): 79–88 [Hebrew].
4 Gross, ibid.
5 Babylonian Talmud, tractate Sanhedrin 4a.
6 Gross, ibid., 7; see *Sefer nitzahon yashan* [The Book of an Old Triumph] (Philadelphia 1976), Hebrew section, paragraph 8, p. 6; Neubauer, "Sources relating the Ten Tribes," 23.
7 Stein Kokin "Toward the Source of the Sambatyon."
8 Neubauer, "Where are the Ten Lost Tribes."

4 Rabbinites and Karaites

The gaon's response to the query from Kairouan:

> On the case of Rabbi Eldad the Danite that you have sent to us ... we have been told by sages that heard from Rabban Isaac ben Mar and Rabban Simcha, who saw this R. Eldad the Danite and were perplexed by his teachings, some of which seemed like the teachings of our sages and some of which ran counter to them.
>
> In contemplating this matter, we have seen passages of our sages that contain support for [the views of Eldad]. According to them, Sennacherib rose forth and exiled the tribes of Zebulun and Naphtali in the eighth year of King Ahaz's reign; and nearly sixty-four years [passed] from the building of the Temple to the eighth [*sic*] year of Ahaz. The Danites, who were brave warriors, realized that the king of Assyria had begun to gain control over Israel. In consequence, they departed from the Land of Israel to Kush and established their residence there, as it was a land of gardens, orchards, fields, and vineyards – an expansive land full of all that is good. They whole-heartedly committed themselves to devoutly worshipping God and lovingly observing all his commandments. This [move] turned out well, as they were endowed with two crowns: Torah and kingdom. All this was related by this same R. Eldad the Danite.
>
> Our rabbis taught that the Jewish people underwent ten exiles: four at the hands of Sennacherib, four at the hands of Nebuchadnezzar, one at the hands of Vespasian, and one at the hands of Hadrian. The tribe of Dan is not mentioned in any of these exiles, for it went off to Kush of its own accord 135 years before the destruction. According to his story, it stands to reason that Dan did not leave until the third exile.

What is more, R. Eldad says that they sentenced [transgressors] to the four capital punishments: stoning, burning, decapitation, and strangulation. As per the rabbis' interpretation, all the executions written in the Torah are without exception strangulation. Furthermore, he says that *bnei Moshe* are [dwelling] next by to them [i.e., the Danites], and they are surrounded by the Sambation River. He was saying the truth, for our sages stated in a midrash that Nebuchadnezzar deported sixty myriad Levites of the *bnei Moshe*. Since they indeed reached the rivers of Babylon, along with their harps, they underwent what R. Eldad told you.

Before our ancestors entered the Land of Canaan, they were preoccupied with wars and forgot the Mishna that they had received from Joshua. They even said of Joshua, may peace be upon him, that he doubts following the death of Moses. Of all the Tribes ... Judah and Benjamin most scrupulously observed the Torah.

Do not be surprised by the variation and substitutions that you heard from the mouth of Eldad, for the sages of Babylon and the sages of the Land of Israel study the same Mishna [albeit] with much revision, to which they [henceforth] neither detract nor add. [Yet] at times, these scholars give one reason and the others a different reason. Like two sages who sit together for the sake of comprehending the Scripture or Mishna, one prefers this reasoning and the other a different reason. Even with respect to the Scripture, which is set down in writing, there are discrepancies between Babylon and the Land of Israel in all that concerns missing and superfluous letters, open and closed portions, accents, and the tradition regarding the end of verses. All the more so with respect to the Mishna, which is enigmatic. Who is capable of encompassing it all?

It bears noting that it is not far-fetched to posit that this Eldad erred and mixed things up due to the profusion of troubles that he endured and the hardships of the road that torment a man's body. At any rate, the Mishna is a unified [work of] law, to which one must neither add nor detract. Moreover, one can admit no changes, be it on matters great or small. The same cannot be said for the Talmud. The Babylonian Jews formulate it in the Aramaic language, and the tongue of the Land of Israel Jews is the Targum (Surasi). On the other hand, the sages that were exiled to Kush studied the Talmud in the Holy Tongue [Hebrew], which they are familiar with. As to the absence of the sages' names [in the Tribes' Talmud], this is because every Mishna that the Jews would interpret in the Temple was generic and did not contain the name of a sage. In any event, there is but one Torah, be it the Mishna or the

Talmud, and everyone drinks from the same well. Moreover, it is ill-advised to interpret everything, for as stated (Proverbs 25:2) "It is the glory of God to conceal a matter."

According to Eldad, they [the Ten Tribes] start off their prayers by blessing first the sages of Babylon and afterwards for the Diaspora *in toto*. This is very good, for most of the sages and prophets were exiled to Babylon, and they established the law, set up residence along the Euphrates River during the reign of King Jeconiah of Judah, [and continue to live there] to this day and age. Furthermore, they were a dynasty of erudition and prophecy, and from them the Torah shall go forth to the entire nation. And we already informed you that everyone drinks from the same well. Steel yourselves with what the sages preach unto you and with the Talmud that they taught you [*sic*], and deviate neither right nor left from all their words, for it is written (Deut. 17:11): "In accordance with the instructions given to you and the ruling handed down to you, thou shalt act."

Picking up where the previous chapter left off, we will elaborate on the historical background of the period in which Eldad's works were produced. More specifically, the ensuing discussion will examine the ideological and political use that was made of the legal (i.e., Halakhic) components of the Danite's oeuvre.

Scholars have long deliberated over which of the Jewish denominations was most closely aligned with Eldad's legal writings (Halakha). In the nineteenth century, following in Alfred Freimann's footsteps, Heinrich Graetz and Adolf Neubauer postulated that he was a Karaite. Neubauer even argued that Eldad was "a cunning emissary of the Karaites." Likewise, he described the Danite as "a deceitful man covered in plots."[1] In the Hebrew edition of Graetz's book, which was translated by S. P. Rabbinowicz and annotated by A. E. Harkavy, the latter two claimed that he was a Rabbinite missionary. For his part, Epstein weighed the possibility that Eldad was a Samaritan. A few similarities aside, he found no basis for this theory.[2]

To truly understand this debate, one must bear in mind that from the ninth century onwards, the Jewish world (primarily its communities in Muslim lands) was sharply divided between the Rabbinites and the Karaites. In contrast to the former, the Karaites deny the authority of the oral law and its representative texts – the Talmuds and Midrashim. While the Karaites possess a tradition of their own, it is directly predicated on the Bible. The two streams were indeed locked in a bitter feud. However, there was also a great deal of contact between its members, which occasionally even triggered cross-pollination. The intra-Jewish strife was not only inter-denominational. Within the Rabbinite world, there was competition over the Diaspora leadership between the Jewish establishments in Babylon (present-day Iraq) and its counterparts in Israel. Furthermore, the two major seminaries in Babylon – *Sura* and *Pumpedita* – vied among themselves for supremacy, as well as the attendant jobs, money, and honorifics.

The researchers who posited that Eldad was a Karaite stressed the glaring differences between his legal traditions and the ninth-century Rabbinite lore (Babylonian and Land of Israel). Owing to these disparities, there was a consensus among the previous generation of scholars that the Danite must be identified with one of the "non-Orthodox" Jewish streams. As such, they looked into the possibility that he was a member of the Samaritans, the Karaites, Ethiopian Jewry, and even communities in China. My own findings point to many similarities with the traditions of the Land of Israel, but the two corpora are certainly not the same (see chapter 5). In a recent paper on the degree of tolerance towards the Other in R. Zemaḥ's response, Adiel Kadari takes the spotlight off the Rabbinite–Karaite dispute and characterizes the adjudicator's response to the Kairouanites as "relatively pluralistic model." Contending with the challenge that Eldad posed to the Rabbinite tradition, the gaon refrained, according to Kadari, from negating the legitimacy of the Lost Tribes' gospel. Instead, he sought to encompass their Torah within the framework of the Rabbinite narrative. In Kadari's estimation, R. Zemaḥ went so far as to introduce a new conception of the Jewish world – a nexus of different centers, each with their own gospel and bona fides.[3]

Indeed, instead of accenting the differences between Eldad's traditions and those of the Rabbintes, let us turn our sights on what the traditions hold in common. Our findings neither reconcile between the two nor conclude that the Rabbinite authorities embraced a pluralistic outlook. In fact, their affinities expose and sharpen the contours of the debate. Accentuating the differences between the two diverts our attention away from the considerable overlap. The similarities are evident before we even delve into the details of Eldad's traditions. Like the Rabbinites in Babylon, Eldad offered a "Talmud," more so one that boasts a direct line to Mount Sinai, thereby strengthening Rabbinite Judaism's argument against Karaism. Although the Danite's gospel indeed contains laws devoid of a source in the known tradition, it is formulated along the lines of the Talmuds that we are familiar with. A case in point is the opening paragraph of his laws of ritual slaughter:

Anyone that sacrifices on behalf of the Jewish people and does
not know *hilkhot shechita* [laws of slaughter], it is forbidden to
eat from his slaughtering. And these are the laws of *shechita*: its
pausings, its pressings, its thrustings, its deflections, and its
tearings ... [4]

This formulation is reminiscent of a corresponding passage in the
Babylonian Talmud:

> Rab Judah stated in the name of Samuel, One may not eat of the
> slaughtering of any butcher who does not know the rules of *she-
> chita*. And these are the rules of *shechita*: pausing, pressing,
> thrusting, deflection, and tearing.[5]

Though we can point to similarities with Karaite laws as well, they did
not have laws of *traifah* (otherwise kosher animals with mortal injuries
or conditions)[6] – a topic that resonates in the parallel Babylonian laws.
Hench, *de facto*, Eldad offered a Talmud and an oral tradition
authenticating the Rabbinite one. Indeed, over the generations, the
Danite's version was comprehended, and indeed wielded, as evidence
against the Karaite worldview.

In his answer to the Kairouanites' query, R. Zemaḥ stressed that
"In contemplating this matter, we have seen passages of our sages that
contain support for [the views of Eldad]." Thereafter, the gaon pointed to sections of Eldad's stories that dovetail neatly with the Midrash
and Talmud. Like the Kairouanites, he emphasized that the Eldad's
laws compromise a "Talmud": "And what you said that the Tribes
have their own Talmud, for the sages that were exiled to Kush with
the Tribes arranged the Talmud for them in the Holy Tongue."[7] In
the process of asserting that Eldad brought a Talmud, the gaon
ordains the Danite with the title of "Rabbi Eldad." He then averred
that the differences between his contemporary Babylonian tradition
and Eldad's laws are limited to marginal issues. In fact, he compared
these discrepancies to those between the Jerusalem and Babylonia
Talmuds:

> Even with respect to the Scripture, which is set down in writing,
> there are discrepancies between Babylon and the Land of Israel in
> all that concerns missing and superfluous letters, open and closed
> portions, accents, and the tradition regarding the end of verses ...
> The Babylonian Jews formulate it in the Aramaic language, and
> the tongue of the Land of Israel Jews is the Targum (Surasi).

Needless to say, the Karaites brought up these differences in their anti-Rabbinite polemic.[8] In R. Zemaḥ's ruling, though, the argument is turned on its head. The discrepancies between the "source" of the Jewish lore – the revelation to Moses on Mount Sinai – and the Babylonian tradition are on a par with the differences between the Babylon and Land of Israel versions of the oral law. That said, the gaon reminded his readers, "there is but one Torah, be it the Mishna or the Talmud, and everyone drinks from the same well."[9]

While R. Zemaḥ implicitly bludgeons the Karaite movement with Eldad's works, they also served another purpose – to reinforce Babylon's position *vis-à-vis* the Land of Israel:

> According to Eldad, they [the Ten Tribes] start off their prayers by blessing first the sages of Babylon and afterwards for the Diaspora *in toto*. This is very good, for most of the sages and prophets were exiled to Babylon, and they established the law, set up residence along the Euphrates River during the reign of King Jeconiah of Judah, [and continue to live there] to this day and age. Furthermore, they were a dynasty of erudition and prophecy, and from them the Torah shall go forth to the entire nation.[10]

It bears noting that the quote attributed to Eldad in the gaon's responsum does not appear in the query from the Kairouanites or any other extant source we possess.

The Karaites themselves also felt threatened by the position latent in Eldad's laws and reacted accordingly. In his work *Eshkol ha-kofer*, Judah Hadassi (a prominent twelfth-century Karaite from Constantinople) incorporated the adventures of "Eldad from the tribe of Dan, disciple of sages" as well as select parts of his description of the Lost Tribes. In Hadassi's estimation, this utopic account, in particular, depicts the Israelites as Karaites: "Their honesty and righteousness in God's Torah, without a Mishna and Talmuds, and the calculation of the moon in months as established by your shepherd [i.e., Karaites]."[11] In other words, despite lacking the Mishna or a Talmud, the Tribes are morally upstanding; and they even set the Hebrew, lunar calendar in the Karaite way. Hadassi's account can thus be viewed as an antithesis of the Rabbinite position, proving from the case of Eldad that the Karaite way is right. At any rate, this version raises an interesting question: Did the Karaite author intentionally change the story, or did it reach his hands devoid of Eldad's Talmud? It is difficult to say. Whatever the case, this is the narrative that was read by Karaite audiences.

The Rabbinite claim turns up in a bevy of revised accounts of the Ten Tribes that were ascribed to Eldad. For instance, quite a few miraculous details were inserted into the storyline, many of which indeed accentuate "the Talmud of the Ten Tribes." The apotheosis of this trend was a rendering that added a single word, "Babylonian," to the accepted version: "And they only know how to speak in the Holy Tongue, and the *Babylonian* Talmud that was laid down by Moses, may peace be upon him, is in their hands."[12] In so doing, the editor equated the gospel of the Lost Tribes with none other than the Babylonian Talmud.

Eldad's radical assertion whereby he possessed the original traditions as transmitted to Moses on Mount Sinai had the potential to undermine the authority of the Talmud's sages and their successors the geonim in Iraq. A look at the details of Eldad's law demonstrates that it was inconsistent with the mainstream oral law in many respects, to the point of seeming to cast doubt on the validity of the Rabbinite tradition. This difference was all the more acute at an hour in which Karaite Judaism was posing what was essentially a very similar challenge to the legitimacy of the oral law and its bearers in Babylon. That said, R. Zemaḥ's assertion that the Lost Tribes have a Talmud was a formidable if tacit defense of the Rabbinite gospel. More specifically, his responsum makes the case that the many and manifold differences *vis-à-vis* the Babylonian Talmud notwithstanding, Eldad's tradition attests to the fact that his own corpus derives from the revelation at Mount Sinai. In the face of the gaon's bold assault, the Karaites had little choice but to strike back. Accordingly, they claimed that in Eldad's testimony, the Lost Tribes did not have any Talmud whatsoever. Having mapped out the assorted versions of these laws and the arguments made by the two adversarial streams, the following question begs asking: Was Eldad a Rabbinite or Karaite? The most viable answer is all of the above, depending on the reader.

Notes

1   Heinrich Graetz, *History of the Jews from the Earliest Times to the Present Day*, the Saul Pinchas Rabbinowicz edition (Warsaw 1896), third volume, 267–274, appendix 19 [Hebrew]; Neubauer, "Where are the Ten Lost Tribes," 109–110.

2   Epstein, 19–20. For more on the Samaritans, see: Hasamein Wasef Kahen, *Samaritan History, Identity, Religion and Subdivisions, Literature and Social Status* (Jerusalem 1966), 27–28.

3   Adiel Kadari, "On Accepting the 'Other' and its Limitations: A Study of the Gaon R. Zemaḥ's Responsa on the Matter of Eldad the Danite," in Uri Ehrlich, Howard Kreisel, and Daniel J. Lasker, eds., *By the Well: Studies in*

Jewish Philosophy and Halakhic Thought Presented to Gerald Blidstein (Beer Sheva 2008), 449–461 [Hebrew].
4 Schloessinger, 58.
5 *Babylonian Talmud*, Hulin, 9a.
6 Nathan Schur, *History of the Karaites* (Jerusalem 2003), 65–66 [Hebrew].
7 As per the Geniza version (Cambridge, T. S Loan 94); Schloessinger, 116–117. The wording of the first print slightly differs; see Epstein, 40.
8 For insights into how the Karaites viewed the discrepancies between the Babylon and Land of Israel traditions, see Zeev Elkin, "The Karaite Version of *Sefer ha-Ḥilluqim bein Benei Erez-Yisrael le-Benei Bavel*," *Tarbiz* 66/1 (October–December 1996): 101–111 [Hebrew].
9 Epstein, 40.
10 Ibid. For more on this matter, see Ben-Sasson, 281–282, including n. 463. As above-noted, Kadari posits that R. Zemaḥ considered various other traditions, namely the Jerusalem Talmud and the Talmud of the Ten Tribes, to be legitimate; Kadari, "On Accepting the 'Other'."
11 Hadassi, *Eshkol ha-kofer*, no. 61, p. 30, column II. For more on Hadassi's description see: Alexander Scheiber, "Eléments fabuleux dans l'Eshkôl Hakôfer de Juda Hadasi," *REJ* 108 (1948): 41–62.
12 This is cited from a sixteenth-century, Italian-language version, which was extracted from MS London, the British Library, Add. 27129. See Müller, 65 (version J).

5 Babylon and Israel

Select examples from Eldad the Danite's laws of ritual slaughter (*shechita*):

> In their laws of *shechita*, they say: Our rabbi Joshua said in the name of Moses in the name of the Almighty, anyone that sacrifices on behalf of the Jewish people who does not know the laws of *shechita*, it is forbidden to eat from his slaughtering. And these are the laws of *shechita*: its pauses, its pressings, its thrustings, its deflections, its [rules concerning] the esophagus, its tears. Here is a disquisition on them:
>
> What is its pauses? A person takes an animal and [while slaughtering it] an emergency comes up, the butcher's knife drops out of his hand or the hood falls over his face, and [in consequence] he pauses for the amount of time it would have taken to complete another slaughter, then the animal is disqualified; and if it takes him less time, it is pure.
>
> What are its pressings? If the butcher's knife is very sharp and he hacks [the gullet and windpipe] in one stroke, the butcher's knife falls on the bone, [or] the [blade] goes back and forth, back and forth, this is pressing ...
>
> What are its thrusts? If the animal hastens to lift its head before being hit by the butcher's knife and the butcher's knife hastily lands between the gullet and the trachea, if it slaughtered above [the trachea], it is appropriate to consume; if it slaughtered below, it is defiled ...
>
> He [i.e., Eldad] told us: We say: Our rabbi Joshua said to Moses our rabbi, What if we find three [lobes] on the left and four on the right [during the post-slaughter inspection of the lungs]? Moses our Rabbi said to him, One day I was in the sanctuary of the Tent of Congregation and I inspected a lung ... [where] I found a fourth

[lobe] stuck to the windpipe. Moreover, I found two livers – one above ... and another beneath the heart – and both of them were stuck together at their outer ends. He [i.e., Moses] instructed them to bring a receptacle of very hot water, and he placed the two livers in a copper utensil. He then poured hot water on them and said: If one [liver] remains intact and the other one dissolves, it [i. e., the animal] is qualified; and if both of them remain intact or both dissolve, it is disqualified ...

He [i.e., Eldad] also said to us: One of the members of our nation came to Joshua and spoke with him: My lord, I am a hunting man; I hunt animals and fowl in the mountains. However, I do not know the signs for distinguishing between defiled and pure. Joshua our rabbi told him: You do not recognize animals that chew their cuds and have split hooves? The hunter told him, [I can detect] an animal with split hooves, but it does not chew its cud in my presence, for I catch them in an abrupt fashion. Our rabbi Joshua told him: This sign will come in handy – if it has upper teeth, it is impure. The hunter told him: My lord, this is on the matter of a beast; what [is the sign] for fowl? Our rabbi Joshua told him: This sign will come in handy when you slaughter it – if it has two lungs and one is connected to the other, it is pure; if it has but one [lung], it is defiled.[1]

In piecing together Eldad's image and place in history, scholars have duly placed a premium on understanding the details of his legal traditions. According to the manuscripts and earliest testimonies, these laws are the oldest works in the Danite's oeuvre. Given their content, peculiarity, and other unique characteristics, these laws are crucial to grasping the man, his place of origin, and place in history. As we have seen, the Kairouanites were most interested in the laws, which were indeed the catalyst behind their query to the gaon.[2] In this chapter, then, we will track the evolution of these laws – especially the omissions and additions that copyists incorporated over the generations – as a main tool in understanding their significance to Jewish culture.

The reconstruction of the Eldadian corpus' evolution opens a window onto a momentous development in the annals of the Jewish people: the rise of the Babylonian Talmud at the expense of all earlier and concurrent Jewish traditions. Our reconstructions points to latent, quiet factors in this victory: the work of scribes and transmitters of texts charged on maintaining tradition but reshaping it in the process. Researchers have pointed to the fact that the shift to Babylonian rule did not transpire overnight. As early as the seventh century, the Babylonian and Land of Israel traditions vied for supremacy. By virtue of adopting new writing strategies, responsa works, massive editing of the Talmud, and above all rabbinical propaganda, the Babylonian lore seized the upper hand. Another key ingredient in this triumph was that the champions of the Babylonian tradition were based in Baghdad – the seat of the Abbasid Dynasty.

By the latter stages of the eleventh century, the entire Jewish world had completely adopted the Babylonian tradition. Of course, not all the Jewish communities embraced its customs at one and the same time. With respect to the northern Mediterranean basin, Robert Bonfil has demonstrated that the Land of Israel Talmud prevailed until the ninth century. The scholarship is divided over when the Babylonian tradition was fully embraced by Ashkenazic (French and German) Jewry.[3] Israel Ta-Shma excavated through layers of the Babylonian culture in the writings of twelfth-century Ashkenazic sages (more on this in chapter 7). He concluded that "the ancient Ashkenaz custom," which leaned heavily on oral traditions from the Land of Israel that had arrived via Byzantium and Italy to Germany, prevailed in the early Middle Ages. Talya Fishman has recently posited that it was only under the influence of the Tosafists (Western European Talmudic commentators between the twelfth and fourteenth centuries) that the Babylonian Talmud became the mandatory law code of the entire Jewish people. In her book, Fishman traces the various stages in this process and argues that even the gaonim of Babylon did not perceive their edifice as the final word in Jewish praxis.[4] By tracking the changes to Eldad's laws of ritual slaughter over the ages, I hope to shed light on this turn of events.

Let us begin with Eldad's presumed arrival to Kairouan. Were the laws that he brought with him in writing or did he share them from memory? The wording of the Jewish community's query suggests that the laws were conveyed in an oral manner: "The following is **said** in every halakha … And he came to **tell** us what is forbidden and permitted … And we found it necessary to unfurl before his eminence [i.e., R. Zemaḥ] this language from their Talmud, a modicum of which we have written." In other words, Eldad spoke and the Kairouanites were the ones to put his laws into writing. The same can be said for a twelfth-century work of Halakha, *Risalat al-Burhan fi Tadhkiyat al-Ḥaiwan*, which was penned in Judeo-Arabic by Samuel ben Jacob ibn Jam'a. One of the most important and earliest eye-witnesses of the wording of the Danite's laws, ibn Jam'a testified that "*wa-nakel* [and **said**] Eldad ben Maḥli." Furthermore, Ḥasdai ibn Shaprut, the famous tenth-century vizier, noted that: "Upon getting up to deliver a sermon on Halakha, he [i.e., Eldad] would **say** … ."[5]

During this period, the oral culture was still in the ascendancy, so that the notion that these laws were conveyed by word of mouth was par for the course. That said, it must be remembered that the era's terminology did not always clearly differentiate between written and oral.[6]

As discussed above, the oldest existing versions of Eldad's laws are two eleventh-century pages from the Geniza (henceforth: Geniza).[7] However, these sources offer but a partial list of them and eschew mentioning the "author." These laws then found their way into ibn Jam'a's above-mentioned work (henceforth: ibn Jam'a).[8] Since ibn Jam'a lived in North Africa and had venerable sources at his disposal, researchers put a premium on this version.[9] What is more, he was the first to explicitly connect these laws of *shechita*, which we are familiar with from later sources, to "Eldad who came from the Ten Tribes."

From the twelfth to the fifteenth century, several lines from the Danite's legal text were the topic of a multigenerational dialogue among the Tosafists and their disciples (discussed in length in chapter 7 below). According to the colophon of the manuscript containing a version of his laws (henceforth: Parma), they were copied in 1289 by one "Shmuel son of R. Yosef the cantor" in Uncastillo.[10] The lines under review bear the title "Laws of Land of Israel."[11] Although Eldad is not explicitly mentioned herein, the phrasing leaves little doubt as to the author's identity: "Laws on slaughter and supervision by Joshua ben Nun who received them from Moses from the Almighty as a decree to Moses from Sinai."

Entire sections of Eldad's laws are also embedded into R. Jacob ben Asher's fourteenth-century book *Arb'a turim* (Four Columns). According to Schloessinger, these passages are the fruit of R. Jacob's hand. Put differently, their appearance in Eldad's prints is the result of a later interpolation.[12] An important, fifteenth-century version of the laws was written on the margins of a manuscript sheet of *Hilkhot ḥulin le-Mordekhai* (The Laws of Animal Slaughter by Moredchai, henceforth: Mordechai's Annotations).[13] In 1480, Abraham Conat published his incunabulum of Eldad's works. Within this framework, the Italian physician-cum-Talmudist summarized the laws that are enumerated in the Kairouanites' letter. Scholars would be hard-pressed to determine the exact relation between all these versions in all that concerns their transmission and copying. However, as we shall see, each of them apparently evolved on an independent basis.

In the pages to come, the full and dated versions of these texts – Geniza, ibn Jam'a, Parma, Mordechai's Annotation, and Conat's incunabulum – will help us ascertain the lingual changes and content revisions that Eldad's laws have undergone over the generations. Thereafter, we will explore the various ways these texts were used between the eleventh and fifteenth centuries. Let us begin by touching on Eldad's own sources.

Epstein and Schloessinger convincingly argue that the Danite's laws are probably not a fabrication. The expertise that this text exhibit in zoology and animal diseases, as well as the details provided and concepts employed, all point to practical knowledge anchored in a concrete reality. By virtue of these findings, both scholars reached similar conclusions: Eldad represents an actual community; and his laws are indicative of its customs. In their estimation, the differences between them and the Babylonian Talmud stem from the fact that his community was quite a distance from Babylon and thus unfamiliar with its traditions. According to Epstein, Eldad was from the southern Arabian Peninsula or East Africa. In addition, he drew an analogy between the community's situation and that of Ethiopian Jewry at the turn of the twentieth century (more on this topic in chapter 8). Schloessinger merely notes that Eldad's place of origin was far removed from the Land of Israel. Nevertheless, his laws share more in common with the tradition of the latter than with the Babylonian tradition.[14]

Among other sources, Epstein compares the Danite's laws to *Halakhot psuqot* (Decreed Laws) – one of the first Gaonic works from the eight century – and shows clear parallels between the two. Working on the assumption that *Halakhot psuqot* was written later, Epstein thus estimated that its author copied the laws under review from Eldad.[15] As it now stands, though, researchers believe that *Halakhot psuqot* dates back to the outset of the Gaonic period ("second half of the eight century, first half of the ninth century"), namely before Eldad's visit to Kairouan.[16] Moreover, they attribute the work to Rabbi Yehudai Gaon and his students (at the same date).[17]

More so, all the similarities between *Halakhot psuqot* and Eldad's laws pertain to the subject of *traifot* (when a slaughtered animal is deemed non-kosher *post mortem*). In essence, Yehudai Gaon's section on *traifot* is not an original part of the book. In the Sassoon manuscript, the most trustworthy, tenth-century manuscript of *Halakhot psuqot*, the section is titled "*Traifot* of the Land of Israel."[18] This heading not only attests to the provenance of these laws, but signifies that they are a short collection tacked on to the book by a copyist. From the standpoint of form and content, researchers found other parallels to Eldad's laws in the Geniza.[19] The points of convergence that Epstein mentioned are taken from this same addition to *Halakhot psuqot*. Therefore, it stands to reason that there was an early source by the name of "*Traifot* of the Land of Israel" containing traditions that resembled those of Eldad. In all likelihood, then, the Danite drew on these or similar laws.[20]

Whether Eldad shared the actual practices of a real community of origin or merely adapted a bundle of laws that he had stumbled upon, the parallels to *"Traifot* of the Land of Israel" and other laws of *shechita* from the Geniza indicate that his laws represent a wider phenomenon: a wide array of religio-legal traditions and praxis that ran counter to the Babylonian lore and, at times, to the Land of Israel tradition as well. These local traditions bear witness to a profusion of customs, methods, and habits. That said, only a small handful of them were put to writing and even fewer have survived into the present era. In this respect, Eldad's laws constitute a rare gem that sheds some light on an obfuscated tradition. These laws, in conjunction with their parallels,[21] demonstrate that besides the two large centers in the Land of Israel and Babylon, small communities sprouted up during this period. These Jewish settlements built their religious life in accordance to multiple factors: their geographical location; the area's material reality; their own lore; and the tradition of their non-Jewish neighbors. The rise of these modest-sized communities engendered a profusion of customs, laws, traditions, and the like. As evidenced by the Kairouanites' letter to R. Zemaḥ, the disparity between these practices and the Babylonian lore already stirred up tensions in late ninth-century North Africa.[22] For this reason, Eldad's laws constitute a revealing remnant of a bygone age. A lack of source material from the "dark age" (of sources) before the tenth century explains the difficulty researchers have in identifying Eldad's laws with a specific Jewish center or denomination. At any rate, his texts have survived by virtue of two factors: their connection to the Ten Lost Tribes, which have sparked the imagination of Jewish readers over the ages; and the special formula "Joshua said in the name of Moses in the name of the Almighty." Hence, their antiquity and rarity provide the perfect grounds to what will follow: tracing the changes that were made to Eldad's laws of *shechita* is likely to help us contend what became of the rich array of customs and traditions that informed the early medieval Jewish world during the next generations.

A close look at the disparities between the various incarnations of Eldad's laws along the chronological axis points to a clear trend: these traditions were gradually adapted, both in terms of language and content, to suit the Babylonian Talmud and normative Halakha. The earliest text, the Geniza version, offers a taste of Eldad's archaic language, which was highly influenced by Biblical Hebrew and the world of sacrifices. A case in point is this short passage from the Geniza: "And were an animal to gore an animal … [S]hould the animal retain its soul [i.e., survive the blow] and stand pure [fully heal], it shall be eaten."[23]

The ibn Jam'a version already contains extensive changes, but these do not alter the core meaning.[24] For instance, the words *tahor* (pure) and *tamei* (defiled) in the Geniza version are replaced with *mutar* (permitted) and *asur* (prohibited), respectively;[25] and instead of *serekh* (adhesion of tissue in the lung), which is unique to Eldad, ibn Jam'a goes with *syrkha*, which bears a resemblance to the language of the sages.[26] "Errors" in masculine and feminine agreement have also been corrected in this version: *nefesh hu* ("he is a soul") is changed to *nefesh hi* ("she is a soul"); and the like. What is more, the archaic *rosheiha* ("her heads") gives way to *rosheah* ("her head"), and the unfamiliar verb *va-ticharkesh* is supplanted by *va-teharev* ("and will become desolate"); this rendering suits, if only barely, the phrase's meaning.[27]

In the Parma version, these changes reached a formidable scale and evince a systematic editing approach. For instance, the above-cited line is basically the same, with the exception of its final clause: "And were an animal to gore an animal ... [if] the animal shall bear its soul, it is kosher." The Biblical tongue is systematically replaced with the language of the sages: *tahor* (clean) and *vlad* (offspring) are supplanted by *kasher* (kosher) and *yeled* (child), respectively; the Aramaic *kuliya* (kidney) replaces the Hebrew *kilyah; arkuvah* (knee), a language-of-the-sages usage, comes instead of *rekhuvah*; the Aramaic *un* (ear) supplants the Hebrew *ozen*; and the preposition *el* (to) is substituted with *etzel* (by); and so on and so forth.[28] This trend is quite pronounced, as even the menacing and coarse "sharp sword" gives way to the more refined and Halakhic "knife."[29] These modifications to the Parma version make it resemble more a work of codification than casuistic law. More specifically, long, detailed, and complicated passages are condensed into general formulae. A passage from the Geniza version, say, reads thus:

> If a person slaughtered from the sheep [family] or from the cattle [family] and found but one kidney, what should he check and see? If it is an ox, he will go to an ox like the one that was slaughtered that same day; and if it is a cow, he should go to a cow like it; and if it is a calf, to a calf like it; and if a young goat, to a young goat ... Then he should take the two kidneys that are found in the animal that is the same kind as his animal and place the two kidneys on the side of a scale and the kidney on the [other] side of the scale. If it stands opposite the two, it is pure and is to be eaten; and if the one pales before the two, it is a *traifah* and is not to be eaten.

In the Parma version, this long explanation has been pared down to "[A]ll the animals [should] be compared to [members of their own species]."[30]

These trends make considerable headway in Mordechai's Annotation, and the content itself is substantially revised. More importantly, Joshua and God are by and large cut out of the quintessential Eldadian opening: "Joshua said in the name of Moses in the name of the Almighty."[31] A typical replacement is "Thus Moses our rabbi taught us." This formula is indeed closer to the popular Mishnaic-Talmudic expression "Halacha to Moses from Sinai." Even where Joshua's name is preserved, the rest of his appellation, ben Nun, is omitted. In consequence, the name can also be understood as referring to R. Joshua from rabbinic literature. This metamorphosis of Eldad's laws indeed breaks new ground with its adaptation into a quasi-Talmudic dialogue.

Last but not least, Abraham Conat's incunabulum meshes Eldad's original laws with Babylonian Talmud texts and normative medieval sources to form an eclectic montage. After careful scrutiny of this version, Schloessinger posited that far-reaching changes were introduced into Conat's version under the sway of Talmudic and Rabbinic works, not least the Babylonian Talmud and the *Arba turim* (section *Yoreh Dai'ah*). According to Schloessinger, the printer added a bevy of interpolations from Rabbinic sources that run counter to Eldad's laws. Conversely, non-legal sections as well as opening, intermediary, and closing remarks were expunged from the original.[32] Succinctly put, the centuries-long transmission process, involving numerous rounds of copying and revisions, slowly but surely transformed Eldad's one-of-a-kind laws into a Babylonian-cum-Rabbinic work by glossing, omitting, and rewriting every trait that was inconsistent with the reigning tradition.[33]

Eldad's laws are a rare remnant from an authentic tradition that dates back to sometime before the ninth century. Though close to the Land of Israel lore, the two are by no means identical. On the other hand, they markedly contravene Babylonian tradition on major issues. The perpetuation of these laws must be ascribed to Eldad's captivating image, the halo of the Ten Tribes, and the laws' direct attribution to Joshua ben Nun, Moshe and the Almighty. Over the course of their transmission, the laws underwent myriad changes. In the final equation, this process was tantamount to adapting these laws to suit the Babylonian tradition and medieval rabbinic conventions. The techniques that copyists availed themselves of for the sake of bringing this metamorphosis to fruition were nuanced and hardly detectable. Among the changes was the masking of the laws' foreign and unique lingual and historical elements; the ensuing replacement of their language with the terminology of Talmudic sages; and eventually the modification of the laws' content. At first, the direct source, "in the name of the Almighty," was obfuscated, and the text was cast, via editing and omissions, into a Talmudic or legal template.

Thereafter, the laws were revised to suit mainstream legal tradition in accordance with the Babylonian Talmud, whereupon they were actually merged with the latter or other normative legal texts from the Middle Ages. While these changes were significant, most of them were executed in an offhand way, be it during the transmission and dissemination of the laws, the editing and writing of books, or within the framework of legal discussions.

In summation, despite the aberrancy of Eldad's laws with respect to language and content, they were integrated into a Babylonian-oriented system of knowledge in an "evolutionary" or cumulative manner. The different versions are not necessarily built in a linear relation one to the other. Additionally, their components were taken from disparate places and eras. Nevertheless, as such, this entire story not only constitutes the annals of the Eldad's laws, but demonstrates a much bigger saga: the homogenization of medieval Jewish civilization into a single, Babylonian-Rabbinic lore. Apart from divulging an earlier tradition that was more legally, stylistically, and mentally diverse, these laws attest to the ways in which this standardization process was carried out. The Land of Israel tradition and other independent frameworks that existed before the 800s were devoured in the Babylonian textual juggernaut. Even the rare vestiges of these erstwhile traditions were assimilated to the point where their unique characteristics were no longer recognizable.

Notes

1 Epstein, 83–87.
2 According to Ben-Sasson, the Kairouanites were able to ascertain whether Eldad's lore was authentic and determined the "nature of his Judaism" via the laws that he revealed to them: Ben-Sasson, 245–246.
3 See the reviews of Avraham Grossman's *The Early Sages of Ashkenaz* (Jerusalem 1981), by Israel Ta-Shema (*Kiryat Sefer* 56,2 [1981]: 344–352), and David Berger (*Tarbiẓ* 53,3 [1984]: 479–487) (both in Hebrew); and the references in the next footnote.
4 Robert Bonfil, "The Cultural and Religious Traditions of French Jewry in the Ninth Century, as Reflected in the Writings of Agobard of Lyons," *Studies in Jewish Mysticism, Philosophy and Ethical Literature, Presented to Isaiah Tishby* (Jerusalem 1986), 327–348 [Hebrew]; idem, "Between Eretz Israel and Babylonia," *Shalem* 5 (1987): 1–30 [Hebrew]; Israel M. Ta-Shma, *Early Franco-German Ritual and Custom* (Jerusalem 1999 [1992]), revised third edition [Hebrew]; Talya Fishman, *Becoming People of the Talmud* (Philadelphia 2011). Haym Soloveitchik holds a thesis that contravenes the above-cited works. Updated English versions of his articles on the topic can be found in: idem, *Collected Essays*, vol. II (Oxford and Portland, OR 2014), 5–215 (esp. chapters 1, 3, 7, 8).

5 Epstein, 38, 100, 121.
6 For more on this topic, see Jacob Sussman, "The Oral Law as Simple as it Sounds: The Power of the Tip of a *Yud*," in idem and David Rosenthal, eds., *Meḥqerei Talmud*, vol. 3/1 (Jerusalem 2005), 209–384 [Hebrew]. It is also possible that other communities Eldad visited put his laws into writing. This, then, would explain both the changes in wording and the abundance of versions.
7 The Taylor-Schechter Collection, Cambridge University, 110 (T. S. Loan 110). This is the basis for Schloessinger's "version A (T-S A)," which includes MS Warsaw – a forgery that I have intentionally left out of this discussion.
8 Samuel ben Jacob ibn Jam'a, *Risalat al-Burhan fi Tadhkiyat al-Ḥaiwan*, MS Oxford, Bodleian Library, 345 MS. Hunt. (Neubauer 793/1). This manuscript is from the thirteenth or fourteenth century. Halacha B in Epstein, Schloessinger: G, version 1. On this author see: Rabbi Samuel ben Jacob Jam'a, *Agur, including an Introduction and a Few Additions to* [Nathan ben Jehiel's] *Sefer ha-arukh*, ed. Salomon Buber, facsimile of the 1888 edition (Jerusalem 1978), 2–9 [Hebrew].
9 Schloessinger, 10–11. Also see Salo W. Baron, *A Social and Religious History of the Jews,* vol. VI, second edition (New York 1958), 221.
10 In Schloessinger's estimation, the Hebrew toponym *On-Castille* refers to Uncastillo – a town in Aragon, Spain; idem, 11. The community scribe (*Scribaria*) of that community is mentioned in a decree issued by King Alfonso III that very same year (1289): J. Régné, *History of the Jews in Aragon: Regesta and Documents, 1213–1327*, ed. Y. T. Assis (Jerusalem 1978), # 2091.
11 We will expand on this topic in the next chapter.
12 Schloessinger, 20.
13 Oxford, Bodleian Library, Opp. 42 (Neubauer 678). Epstein, halakha 4; Schloessinger, version A, p. 79 ff.
14 Epstein, 6–7, 9–12, 26–33; Schloessinger, 46–48.
15 Epstein, 200–204. To this point, the only extant version of *Halakhot psuqot* was the one published by Schlusberg (Versailles 1886).
16 Robert Brody, *Readings in Geonic Literature* (Tel Aviv 1998), 115 [Hebrew].
17 Neil Danzig, *Introduction to Halakhot Pesuqot* (New York 1993) [Hebrew]
18 Rav Jehudai Gaon, *Sefer Halachot Pesuqut*, codex Sasson 263, a limited facsimile edition of 200 copies, introduction by Shraga Abramson (Jerusalem 1971), 297 [Hebrew]; *Halakhot psukot*, S. Sassoon edition, Makize Nirdamim (Jerusalem 1951), 193 [Hebrew]. An image of the page with this title can be found on p. 30.
19 Ibid., 27–28; Danzig, *Introduction to Halakhot Pesuqot*, 84; J. N. Epstein, "The Lore of Erez Israel: Traifot," *Tarbiẓ* 2/3 (April 1931): 308–318, esp. 312–313, 314, n. 3; 315, n. 2 and 6; 318, n. 14 [Hebrew].
20 Bonfil, "The Cultural and Religious Traditions of French Jewry," 339–346; M. Margulies, *Land of Israel Halakhas from the Geniza* (Jerusalem 1973), 95, 107 [Hebrew].
21 For instance, ibn Jam'a was the first to quote from Eldad's laws. Moreover, he is among the writers that drew on "*Traifot* of the Land of Israel," which he mostly referred to as *Hilkhot reu*. Ibn Jam'a's version bears a resemblance to those in *Halakhot psuqot* and to the portions from the Geniza

published by J. N. Epstein, "The Lore of Erez Israel: Traifot." For other
parallels, see Danzig, *Introduction to Halakhot Pesuqot*, 609–613, n. 5, 8,
18, 20, 27, 28, 33, 38.

22 Ben-Sasson notes that scholars would be hard-pressed to reconstruct what
occurred before the ninth century; idem, 402–404.

23 Schloessinger, 69, §17.

24 It is evident that the Geniza version was not at ibn Jam'a's disposal, for the
two texts share only three paragraphs in common. These differences hinder
our ability to compare these versions.

25 Schloessinger, 86, §36.

26 Ibid., 65, §9e.

27 Ibid., 86, §36. For a possible definition of *va-ticharkesh*, see ibid., 34.

28 Ibid., 65, §9. With respect to the words *ozen* and *una*, see ibid., n. 61; and J.
N. Epstein, "The Lore of Erez Israel," 318, n. 14.

29 Schloessinger, 65, §9e.

30 Ibid., 70–71, §20. Other examples can be found in ibid., 72, §23 (n. 238a);
73, §23 (n. 243); 82, §33c.

31 In Schloessinger's eclectic version, the formula "Our rabbi Joshua said in
the name of Moshe in the name of the Almighty" appears in its entirety
but once; ibid., 84, §34.

32 Ibid., 19–25.

33 Sussmann points to similar "Babiylonisation" of classical Palestinian texts:
Jacob Sussmann, "The Ashkenazi Yerushalmi MS — 'Sefer Yerushalmi',"
Tarbiẓ 66, 1 (1995): 37–63 [Hebrew].

6   Men and women

Mishna (2nd century CE), tractate Hulin, 1:1

> Everyone may slaughter and their slaughtering is kosher, except for
> a deaf person, an imbecile, and minor, lest they botch [the job].

Tosafot (12th century, France) gloss on Babylonian Talmud, Hulin, 2a

> "Everyone may slaughter": It is written in "the Laws of the Land
> of Israel" that women should not slaughter, for their minds are
> frivolous. However, this does not appear to be the case, for they
> are allowed even to slaughter sacrifice in the temple (*kodashim*) to
> begin with (*le-khatchila*) as stated in the chapter [beginning with
> the words] *Kol ha-psulin*, All those that are ineligible who have
> [nevertheless] slaughtered, *diavad* [in hindsight], yea [i.e., the
> slaughter is valid] and *le-khatchila*, nay.

Mordechai Ben Hillel (d. 1298, Germany) *Annotations on Hulin*, 1:1

> "Everyone may slaughter": It appears that it was not said here [in
> tractate Hulin that there is] "One [rule] for men and one for
> women," as it is evident that a woman is fit to slaughter even from
> the outset [and even] with respect to *kodashim* [holy slaughter of
> sacrifice in the temple]. It is said in the chapter [beginning with the
> words] *Kol ha-psulin* ["All the ineligible"] that slaughtering is per-
> mitted for women and non-Jews.
>   Our Rabbi Baruch wrote: I saw it written in the laws of slaughter
> that were brought by Rabbi Eldad ben Maḥli who hails from the Ten
> Tribes: "Joshua said in the name of Moses in the name of the
> Almighty, Anyone that offers a sacrifice to God and knows not
> the laws of slaughter, it is forbidden to eat from his slaughtering and

the like, to the point where Joshua said that any butcher who per-
forms a slaughter that is unsuitable, be it a domesticated animal, a
wild animal, or a fowl, it is an abomination. He must not eat and
slaughter until he turns [in the direction of] the holy [Jewish
Temple] as [is customary] during prayers. And if he slaughters
without a blessing, it is an abomination; and if he slaughters in the
nude and if he is inebriated, it is an abomination; and if he
slaughtered and he did not have on a hood, it is an abomination;
and if he was not cleansed of semen and forgot and slaughtered, it
is an abomination. Furthermore, it is prohibited to slaughter
while ... [in] mourning. In addition, the hands of a woman, the
hands of a eunuch, the hands of an old man whose eightieth year
has passed him by, and a youth who has yet to reach his eighteenth year are forbidden from partaking in [the act of] slaughter."
Heretofore, we have cited from Eldad's words. But all these things
are merely an extra stringency, and we do not conduct ourselves in
this fashion.

The Mishna, the most elementary Halakhic text, permits women to
slaughter animals for the sake of consumption (i.e., *shechitat ḥulin* or
profane butchering). From a modern perspective, the very idea of a
woman engaged in slaughter triggers conflicting images: the delicate
woman *vis-à-vis* the brutality of this act; and the deadly blade *vis-à-vis*
the life-giving woman. On the one hand, slaughtering is tied to the
preparation of food and the kitchen – sole preserves of the medieval
and early modern woman. On the other, it is a ritual that entails
complex legal knowledge and procedures – a seemingly "masculine"
undertaking. The present chapter touches on the historic mutations of
these stipulations and endeavors to ascertain the role of the Eldadian
literature in the changes to the Jewish woman's standing at the close
of the Middle Ages. In this sense, reconstructing the various stages in
the transmission of the Danite's writing falls under the purview of
gender studies.

We will open with the sources: according to the Mishna then,
women were permitted to slaughter. At the end of the fifteenth century, though, a custom forbidding women to engage in this field
reared up. Soon enough, it became a prevalent and obligatory norm
in the vast majority of Ashkenazic communities. This shift dovetails
neatly with the scholarship of Avraham Grossman and Elisheva
Baumgarten who point to the social diminution of women at the
twilight of the Middle Ages, not least their mounting exclusion from
religious life.[1]

In practice, women probably slaughtered animals over the entire medieval period.[2] During the twelfth century, though, we find exceptions to this rule. A case in point is the excerpt from the Tosafot brought at the outset of this chapter citing "the Laws of the Land of Israel."[3] A generation or two later, "Our Rabbi Baruch" (apparently none other than Baruch of Mainz, ob. 1221) cited "laws of slaughter brought by Rabbi Eldad ben Maḥli who hails from the Ten Tribes" that debar women from this activity: " ... the hands of a woman, the hands of a eunuch, the hands of an old man whose eightieth year has passed him by, and a youth who has yet to reach his eighteenth year are forbidden from partaking in [the act of] slaughter." Be that as it may, Rabbi Baruch immediately characterized this injunction as an "extra stringency" that is no longer in practice. Over the course of the thirteenth and fourteenth centuries, a handful of other adjudicators issued similar opinions.[4] Meir of Rothenburg (1220–1293) vigorously dismissed the practical relevance of the Eldadian corpus:

> On the [matter of] slaughter by women, can they [engage in such activities]? It is already evident from tractate *Zevaḥim* that slaughter is permitted for women, even to begin with ... And that which is cited from the "Laws of the Land of Israel" [is brought] by those who want to innovate and who "rejoice in a thing of nought" (according to Amos, 6:13).[5]

At the latter stages of the medieval period, Jewry changed its attitude towards female slaughter. R. Asher ben Yeḥiel (ob. 1327), a renowned Talmudist, continued along the lines of his mentor Meir of Rothenburg. By the fifteenth century, though, the custom prohibiting women to slaughter had already taken root. The ensuing words of R. Jacob ben Judah Landau, a fifteenth-century Halakhic scholar in North Italy widely referred to as *ha-Agur*, epitomizes this *volte-face*:

> It is self-evident that a woman is fit to slaughter, even from the outset and even *kodahsim* ... [But] it is customary throughout the Jewish Diaspora that they should not slaughter, and I have never seen a custom [allowing women] to slaughter. Therefore, one should not let them slaughter, for the custom overrides the law, and the custom of our ancestors is as valid as the Torah.[6]

Landau's words, which must be a faithful account of the practice at the time, attest to the fact that he was familiar with the medieval discourse, including the Tosafists' ruling. Nonetheless, he rejected their opinion in

favor of a custom that had spread "throughout the Jewish Diaspora."
Owing to the adjudication of R. Moses Isserles (Krakow, 1530–1572),
this custom was adopted far and wide.[7]

Against this backdrop, the following questions beg asking: What
sparked this reversal between the time of the R. Asher and R. Landau?
And if this was indeed a "custom of our ancestors," how come the
Tosafists have shrugged it off without reservations?

For the sake of answering these questions, we will start out by
examining the origins of this stricture. The sources above suggest that
female slaughter was already the object of debate in the Middle Ages.
The Tosafists and, all the more so, Meir of Rothenburg mentioned an
opinion deriving from the "Laws of the Land of Israel" that forbids
such activity. Insofar as Meir of Rothenburg was concerned, the sup-
porters of this injunction were circulating a serious call to action in an
effort "to innovate" and to "rejoice in a thing of nought."

Let us turn our attention to the provenance of the "Laws of the Land
of Israel." The successors to the Tosafists in Ashkenaz – foremost
among them R. Baruch of Mainz[8] – and even modern researchers[9]
identified these laws with those of Eldad the Danite. In fact, the prohibition under review surfaces in a version of Eldad's legal writings that
can be found in a manuscript from 1289 (above mentioned: Parma):[10]

> And this slaughter is off limits to a blind person, [...] an amputee,
> [... and] a leper and is unacceptable [if performed] in the dark.
> However, in the sun, in moonlight, and when a candle is raised
> [*sic*], it is permitted ... If the slaughter is carried out by a woman,
> [...] a congenitally impotent man, [...] a youth who should not
> slaughter until he has reached eighteen years, and by ... an elderly
> person over the age of eighty on account of which his strength has
> left him, [for] he has difficulty collecting his thoughts, his hands are
> trembling, and the butcher's knife sways in his hand, then he will
> not have achieved a permissible slaughter [*sic*].[11]

Following in the footsteps of Graetz, Reifmann, and Epstein, most
scholars contend that the Tosafists' name for Eldad's laws – Laws of
the Land of Israel (*hilkhot Eretz-Yisrael*) – was the outgrowth of an
error. More specifically, the Tosafists dubbed Eldad's laws *hilkhot amar
Yehoshua* on account of their opening words, thereby giving rise to the
corresponding acronym *hei, lamed, alef, yod*. Sometime later, a copyist
misinterpreted this acronym as standing for *hilkhot Eretz Yisrael*.[12] In
all that concerns the manuscripts at our disposal, though, this hypothesis is unfounded. Consequently, there is no reason to stray from the

literal meaning and invent a nonexistent acronym. What is more, as noted by Max Schloessinger, the editor of these laws, the phrase *amar rabbeinu Yehoshua* ("our rabbi Joshua said") appears in most of the versions of Eldad's laws; and the word *rabbeinu* naturally obviates the acronym *alef-yod*. [13]

As discussed earlier, J. N. Epstein discerned the close resemblance between the Danite's laws and the Land of Israel tradition back in 1931.[14] As mentioned in the last chapter, he showed that another early source, "*Traifot* of the Land of Israel," is, at the very least, highly reminiscent of Eldad's halakhic writing. In light of the above, then, the Tosafists either dubbed Eldad's laws "the Laws of the Land of Israel" on their own, on the basis of a genuine resemblance between them. Or an actual treatise of Laws of Slaughter arrived to them from the Land of Israel in an independent manner. If so, the identification with the Danite's Laws, based on some similarities, was only made a generation later.

How are we to understand the very essence of the prohibition against female slaughter? As discussed earlier, among the hallmarks of Eldad's Laws of Slaughter are that they narrow the gap between profane and sacred slaughter.[15] For instance, he disqualified items that were slaughtered without a blessing or hood and by butchers who had *keri* (the release of semen during nocturnal emission). As Abraham Epstein observed, this explanation can help solve a number of problems with Eldad's approach. However, the Danite did not explicitly mention why women have been disbarred from the field of slaughter. What we do know is that he broached the subject of women in the middle of a paragraph that commences with the topic of *temei'im* (people who ritually are unfit for slaughter because they are impure) and ends with a discussion on infirmities that preclude butchers from engaging in their vocation.[16] Against this backdrop, it stands to reason that the injunction against women is tied to Eldad's approximation of profane slaughter with Temple-era sacrifice. Within this context, women are deemed to be both weak and impure. Likewise, menstruation inalterably disqualifies women from serving as butchers and renders them inferior to men. For the most part, this stricture is indicative of a religious sense of taboo and revulsion or a spontaneous, emotionally-driven rejection. Such feelings tend to be expressed and brought to fruition in the meta-Halakhic realm of custom (*minhag*).[17]

Hence, the opposition to female slaughter is part and parcel of an overarching worldview that rests on the following pillars: a strong affinity with the Land of Israel tradition that is manifest in, among other things, the ascription of sacredness to profane realms; stringent practices that go beyond what is formally required by Law; a penchant for folk customs;

and last but not least, a metaphysical aversion to corporeality in general and the female body in particular.

This account dovetails neatly with the findings of Israel Ta-Shma on Northern European Jewish culture in the tenth century, which he refers to as "early Ashkenazic custom." Predicating itself on the Land of Israel's tradition, from which it is partially derived, this custom, in Ta-Shma's estimation, gave voice to religious feelings. What is more, it centered around a wide assortment of notions and practices that today would be classified as superstitions: demonology, dream interpretation, folk medicine, and the like. This worldview also features a metaphysical attitude towards the body (especially that of the woman) and somatic processes, like menstruation and *keri*, as well as a preference for custom over deductive rulings.[18] As per these scholars, the old Ashkenazic tradition ultimately ceded the stage to the Babylonian Talmud in the tenth or eleventh century. This turn of events ushered in a written code and systematic lore, both of which were articulated by the geonim in Babylon. Talya Fishman notes that the Babylonian Talmud's victory over the European tradition culminated in the logic-based enterprise of the Tosafists.[19] Ta-Shma describes an inverse relation between the old Ashkenazic custom and the Tosafists' movement. During the opening stages of the Babylonian Talmud's westward expansion, Ashkenazic adjudicators buttressed the standing of local custom. However, the ascension of the Tosafists whittled away at this lore, while pointing it out for future historians.[20]

In the previous chapter, we indeed retraced this process through the lens of textual tradition of Eldad's legal code. This struggle is exemplified by the twelfth- and thirteenth-century dispute pitting the Tosafists and their successors against the proponents of the laws of the Danite and those of the Land of Israel. Needless to say, the Tosafists' exegetical literature can be defined as having a more rational-legalist perspective whose main source of authority is the Babylonian Talmud. With respect to the matter at hand, the Tosafists rejected the "Land of Israel" prohibition against female slaughter by dint of a *kal va'chomer* (*Argumentum a fortiori*): since the Babylonian Talmud allows women to butcher *kodashim* (sacrifices), it is only logical that this same ruling applies to profane contexts. Needless to say, this sort of reductive logic is among the hallmarks of the Babylonian Talmud. And the same can also be said for Christian scholasticism, which holds much in common with the Tosafist approach.[21]

While there are other facets to the Babylon–Israel rivalry, it undoubtedly entailed a collision between two schools of thought that were at odds on several fronts: custom versus written law; mysticism versus legalism; religious ardor versus legalistic rationalism; and the legacy of the past versus an intellectual predilection for renewal.

Who, then, were the forces manning either side of the barricades? As we have seen, the legalists were clearly the Tosafists in France and their German successors.[22] However, we can only surmise as to the identity of their adversaries. Haym Soloveitchik has demonstrated that the rise of the Tosafists was accompanied by social tension. In consequence, he suggests that the group of German Pietists (*Ḥasidei Ashkenaz*) sought to counter their rationalist counterparts and restore the old balance of power.[23] But this can serve only as a hypothesis.

The picture that seems to be emerging from the literature is that there was indeed an age-old custom in Ashkenaz whereby slaughter was off-limits to women. In all likelihood, this prohibition derived from a tradition in and around the Land of Israel that was bolstered by an Eldadian tradition and its direct transmission from "the Almighty." However, the spread of the Babylonian approach and texts led to the termination of this stricture, at least in certain circles. At some point, the defenders of the Land of Israel's tradition – whomever they may be – endeavored to revive this custom. The up-and-coming Tosafists, though, aspired to dictate a culture that revolved around the Babylonian way (coinciding with the rise of Christian scholasticism in Northern France during this same period). By virtue of their unflagging commitment to Mishnaic law, the Jewish proponents of deductive reasoning vehemently objected to the prohibition against female slaughter.[24]

Contrary to what one can expect, but not surprising to anyone familiar with the Tosafists,[25] the latter's justification is that this is the custom across Ashkenazic communities allowing female slaughter. In contrast, the factors that opposed such "leniency" surprisingly drew on a written source of authority: "the Laws of the Land of Israel." To reiterate, Meir of Rothenburg referred to this camp as "those who want to innovate." It bears noting that the medieval mindset was averse to change and, all the more so, to destroying the old. Therefore, some adjudicators went so far as to label Eldad's halakhic approach as one of "added stringency."[26] In other words, they did not completely reject the Danite's position, but tried to hold both ends of the stick at one and the same time: Eldad's laws are neither "incorrect" nor do they contravene the Babylonian Talmud. This opinion took a foreign law – the prohibition against female slaughter – and imbedded it into an accepted theoretical and terminological framework that distinguishes between mandatory law and optimal stringency.

Let us now proceed to the late Middle Ages. From whence did the custom prohibiting female butchers materialize during the lifetime of the Agur (ob. 1493)? While rationalism was on the decline, mystical thought was commensurately spreading its wings throughout Europe.

Likewise, there was a resurgence in folk customs, such as the prohibition against female slaughter, at the expense of the written code.[27] These developments were perhaps a reaction within Ashkenazic Jewry to the enormous strides made by the Tosafists and their ideology. In fact, the advance of mysticism is embodied in this same injunction. By embracing the argument of "the custom of our ancestors" and denying that Jewish women were engaged in such activities, Landau was associating himself with the old Ashkenazic lore.[28]

In all likelihood, the Agur's ruling betokens a shift in the Jewish conception of profane slaughter. From a quotidian religious act governed by normative rules, it became a ritual endowed with metaphysical significance (as it was in the Laws of Eldad and the "Land of Israel"). This development pushed slaughter in the direction of a ritual act, like sacrifice. As such, it is only logical that Jewish butchers should undergo special purification rituals, examples of which can be found in Eldad's writings. Not surprisingly, then, sections of a corpus that pertain to *hilkhot shechita* (laws of slaughter) were assembled in a fourteenth-century manuscript edition of *Sefer Ḥasidim* (Book of the Pious) under the heading: "Matters of Slaughter, Purity, and Asceticism."[29] Accordingly, women were excluded from such activities because they were perceived as immutably defiled by menstruation.[30]

Be that as it may, categorizing this injunction as the renewal of a bygone custom is insufficient. There is little doubt that this process is tied to developments in contemporaneous Christian society, like the rise of folk customs, the strengthening of rituals, and a major uptick in the exclusion of women from religious life.[31] Moreover, it stemmed from socio-economic processes that were sweeping through all of Western Europe – both the region's Jewish and non-Jewish sectors alike. A case in point is the professionalization of animal slaughter at the tail end of the Middle Ages. Commencing in the twelfth century, this process steadily intensified over the next 300 years. Within this framework, community leaders appointed salaried butchers from among candidates that had passed a test on the laws of slaughter. To some degree, elements of this phenomenon also informed earlier periods. However, by the dawn of the sixteenth century, the communal butcher was granted an official certificate that reinforced his veritable monopoly over this field.

Once more, Landau was among the first Jewish legal authorities to spell out this new reality: "In Ashkenaz it is customary not to rely on the slaughterer unless he has permission to do so from a sage that had tested and confirmed [that the examinee was versed] in the laws of slaughter and butchered 3 fowls in his presence."[32] With respect to the certificate, it was R. Moses Isserles who filled in the blank:

Therefore, it is customary that a person does not slaughter unless he received approval from a sage. And the sage does not give him approval until ascertaining that he knows the laws of slaughter and is proficient with the hand [*sic*]. Therefore, it is customary that we trust everyone that is active in slaughter from the outset. And we do not check them at the beginning or end, for everyone that is on record as a [practitioner of the trade of] slaughtering already received approval from a sage. In a few places, they are habitually stricter, for the recipient is furnished a written document ... as proof that he [i.e., the sage] gave him approval.[33]

As part of this "reform," novice butchers were required to undergo Halakhic-cum-professional training and pass both a theoretical and practical test in order to attain official certification. Needless to say, women had long been excluded from higher educational frameworks, as learning was deemed to be a patently masculine field. Likewise, the examination – the display of knowledge before men – was considered inappropriate for women, whose "dignity," so it was thought, "rests within." For the most part, the professionalization of slaughter moved this activity from the home to the marketplace, which was gradually becoming an exclusively male realm. This transformation reflects an outlook according to which women should be relegated to the domestic sphere.[34]

The exclusion of women from this field, like other rituals, certainly had a negative impact on their place in society. Be that as it may, this state of affairs was not as categorical as it seems. At times and certain places, new socio-economic constraints thrust women into a greater public role. In Italy, for instance, where butcher permits were granted to Jewish women from the sixteenth century.[35] Not only was there an established tradition of female slaughter in Italy, but as pointed out by Robert Bonfil, there was a need to allow women to slaughter: Italian Jewry was scattered among a bevy of small communities, for Jews had settled in small, backwater towns with few co-religionists in their midst. As a result, most of these collectives lacked the wherewithal to hire a professional butcher.[36] For the sake of conducting full Jewish lives in isolated environments, young women and even children were encouraged to learn the trade. Distinguished rabbis tested the women's theoretical and practical competence in this field, and endowed them with a written certificate. In sum, unlike other communities, the traditions and unique socio-economic conditions that informed Italian Jewry stood behind the relative gender equality in the field of profane slaughter.

A survey of the various incarnations of Eldad's prohibition on women acting as kosher slaughters aligned several sets of dichotomies, medieval and modern; men and women; holy and profane; and private and public. The move from the Middle Ages into the early modern time saw a revival of the ancient attitudes of ritual and the sacred, such as Eldad's. This brought to the exclusion of women from religious life, while the rise of the domestic-market dichotomy at the onset of the modern era also spawned a feminine–masculine divide. Nevertheless, as in Italy though, socio-economic realities occasionally brook the divide between these dichotomies. In this case, demographic, economic, and cultural realities propelled women out from the domestic realm into the male-dominated public sphere, allowing them to gain education and written certificates.

Notes

1 Avraham Grossman, *Pious and Rebellious: Jewish women in Medieval Europe*, Jonathan Chipman (tr.) (Waltham, MA 2005), 277–281; Elisheva Baumgarten, *Mothers and Children: Jewish family life in Medieval Europe* (Princeton 2004), 185–189.
2 This hypothesis is substantiated by Grossman, ibid., 190–191. For more on this topic, see Daniel Sperber, *Minhagei Yisrael: Origins and History*, vol. IV (Jerusalem 1995), 9–11; vol. VI, 260–263 [Hebrew]; Salo W. Baron, *The Jewish Community: Its History and Structure to the American Revolution*, vol. II (Philadelphia 1942), 107; Charles Duschinsky, "May a Woman Act as Shoheteth?" in Bruno Schindler (ed.), *Occident and Orient. Gaster Anniversary Volume* (London 1936), 96–106. The pertinent sources unexpectedly refrain from distinguishing between the slaughter of fowl and meat.
3 *Babylonian Talmud*, Ḥulin, 2b, section beginning "All may slaughter." A similar passage surfaces in Zevaḥim, 31b, section beginning "All the ineligible who slaughtered."
4 *Ohr zaruah*, part I, Laws of Slaughtering, §367; *ROSh* [R. Asher ben Yeḥiel], Ḥulin, chap 1:1.
5 *Responsa of the MaHaRaM of Rothenburg*, part IV, 193 (Ms. Munich, §149).
6 *Sefer ha-Agur*, Laws of Slaughter, 1:62.
7 *Hagahot haRaMA* [Gloss of R. Moses Isserles], Shulchan Arukh, Yoreh De'ah, Laws of Slaughter, 1:1.
8 For more on this figure, see Simcha Emanuel, "Rabbi Baruch of Mainz – Portrait of a Scholar as Reflected in the Fragments of His Writings," in *Issues in Talmudic Research, Conference Commemorating the Fifth Anniversary of the Passing of Ephraim E. Urbach, 2 December 1996* (Jerusalem 2001), 124–163 [Hebrew]; idem, *Fragments of the Tablets: Lost Books of the Toasaphists* (Jerusalem 2006), 104–153 [Hebrew].
9 Epstein, 147.
10 Ms. Parma (De Rossi, 327) encompasses this version of the Danite's laws.
11 Schloessinger, 78; Epstein, 134.
12 Epstein, 147.
13 Schloessinger, 51, n. 1.

14 J. N. Epstein, "The Lore of Erez Israel: Traifot."
15 Epstein, 26–33.
16 For the full version, see the discussion above.
17 Baumgarten discusses this tradition, its strictures pertaining to women, and the Land of Israel sources behind these constraints. In addition, she compares this worldview to its Christian analogue. Baumgarten, "'And They do Nicely': A Reappraisal of Menstruation. Women's Refusal to Enter the Sanctuary in Medieval Ashkenaz," in Avraham Reiner et al., *Ta Shma: Studies in Memory of Israel M. Ta-Shma* (Alon Shevut, Israel 2011), 85–104 [Hebrew].
18 Israel Moshe Ta-Shma, *Early Franco-German Ritual and Custom*, 61–74, 86, 98–103. Idem, "On Some Franco-German *Nidda* Practices," *Sidra* 9 (1993): 164–170 [Hebrew]; also published in his *Ritual, Custom and Reality in Franco-Germany, 1000–1350* (Jerusalem 1996), 280–288 [Hebrew].
19 Talya Fishman, *Becoming People of the Book.*
20 Ta-Shma, *Early Franco-German Ritual*, 86, 95–98.
21 For a summary of the different views concerning the relation between the Tosafist movement and scholasticism, see Ta-Shma, *Talmudic Commentary in Europe and North Africa: Literary History*, first part: 1000–1200, revised second edition (Jerusalem 1999), 84–89 [Hebrew].
22 Meir of Rothenburg played an interesting role in this process. As Baumgarten demonstrates, this ruling is indicative of a thirteen-century trend constricting women's participation in religious life. Baumgarten, *Mothers and Children*, 90–91.
23 Haym Soloveitchik, "Three Themes in *Sefer Hasidim*," *AJS Review* 1 (1976): 311–357.
24 Ta-Shma outlines a similar dispute in idem, *Early Franco-German Ritual*, 88–90.
25 Haym Soloveitchik, *Halakha, Economy, and Self-Image* (Jerusalem 1985), 111–112 [Hebrew]; idem, "Rupture and Reconstruction: The Transformation of Contemporary Orthodoxy," *Tradition* 28/4 (1994): 67.
26 *Ohr zaruah*, part I, Laws of Covering Blood, § 387; *ROSh*, Hulin, I, § 1; *Responsa of the ROSh*, rule 48, § IV. The explanation whereby the difference between an existing tradition and one brought forth by Eldad Danite stemmed from an added stringency is also prevalent in his stories of the Ten Tribes. See Müller, 65.
27 Yedidya Alter Dinari, *The Rabbis of Germany and Austria at the Close of the Middle Ages* (Jerusalem 1984), chapter 15 [Hebrew]; Ta-Shma, *Early Franco-German Ritual*, 19, including the references to his scholarship in n. 11 therein.
28 In Salo Baron's synopsis on this topic, he discussed the influence of the Eldadian/Land of Israel Laws on the revival of this prohibition over the course of "several centuries of hesitation"; idem, *The Jewish Community*, vol. II, 107.
29 *Sefer Hasidim,* Ms. Parma, H 3280, before § 1649; and the Wistineski edition, 400.
30 It is impossible to determine what came first: the perception of women as impure or the notion that the act of slaughtering requires a special purification regimen. That said, it is evident that this custom was a product of the encounter between these outlooks towards the ends of the Middle Ages.

31 Dinari examines the enhanced standing of customs in both Jewish and Christian society during this period; idem, *The Rabbis of Germany*, 225–228.
32 *Sefer ha-Agur*, Laws of Slaughter, 1:63.
33 *Gloss of R. Moses Isserles*, Shulchan Arukh, Yoreh Dai'ah, Laws of Slaughter, 1:1.
34 David Herlihy notes that professionalization was one of the factors behind the exclusion of women from the work force during the latter stages of the medieval period; idem, *Opera Muliebria: Women and Work in Medieval Europe* (Philadelphia 1990), 188–190.
35 For a discussion on butcher permits for women, see Duschinsky, "May a Woman Act as Shoheteth," 102–106; Yosef Zuriely, "Ritual Sheḥita by Women: Halakha and Practice," *Proceedings of the World Congress of Jewish Studies* II (division C, 1993): 169–176 [Hebrew]; idem, "Slaughtering Approvals for Women," in Joseph Dahuh Halevi, ed., *Mabuei Afikim* (Tel Aviv 1995), 313–323 [Hebrew]; idem, "Permission for Women to Slaughter: A Safeguard within a Safeguard," *Hagigai Giv'ah* 3 (1995): 91–99 [Hebrew].
36 Robert Bonfil, "The Historian's Perception of the Jews in the Italian Renaissance: Toward a Reappraisal," *REJ* 143 (1984): 59–82, esp. 71–75.

7 Jews and Christians

From Prester John's letter (c. 1165):

John, priest by the almighty power of God and the might of our Lord Jesus Christ, King of Kings and Lord of Lords, to his friend Emanuel, prince of Constantinople, greeting, wishing him health, prosperity, and the continuance of divine favor ... I, Presbyter Johannes, the Lord of Lords, surpass all under heaven in virtue, in riches, and in power; seventy-two kings pay us tribute ... In the three Indies our magnificence rules, and our land extends beyond India, where rests the body of the holy apostle Thomas; it reaches towards the sunrise over the wastes, and it trends toward deserted Babylon near the Tower of Babel. Seventy-two provinces, of which only a few are Christian, serve us. Each has its own king, but all are tributary to us. Our land is the home of elephants, dromedaries, camels, crocodiles, meta-collinarum, cametennus, tensevetes, wild asses, white and red lions, white bears, white merules, crickets, griffins, tigers, lamias, hyenas, wild horses, wild oxen, and wild men – men with horns, one-eyed men, men with eyes before and behind, centaurs, fauns, satyrs, pygmies, forty-ell high giants, cyclopses, and similar women. It is the home, too, of the phoenix and of nearly all living animals. We have some people subject to us who feed on the flesh of men and of prematurely born animals, and who never fear death. When any of these people die, their friends and relations eat him ravenously, for they regard it as a main duty to munch human flesh. Their names are Gog, Magog, Anie, Agit, Azenach, Fommeperi, Befari, Conei-Samante, Agrimandri, Vintefolei, Casbei, and Alanei. These and similar nations were shut in behind lofty mountains by Alexander the Great, towards the north ... Our land streams with honey and is overflowing with milk. In one region grows no poisonous herd, nor does a querulous frog ever quack in it; no scorpion exists, nor does the serpent glide amongst the grass, not can any poisonous animals exist in it or injure anyone ... At the foot of Mount Olympus bubbles up a spring which changes its flavor hour by hour, night and day, and the spring is scarcely three days' journey from Paradise, out of which Adam was driven. If anyone has tasted thrice of the fountain, from that day he will feel no fatigue, but will, as long as he lives, be as a man of thirty years ... All riches, such as are upon the world, our Magnificence possesses in superabundance. With us, no one lies, for he who speaks a lie is thenceforth regarded as dead – he is no more thought of or honored by us. No vice is tolerated by us. The Amazons and the Brahmins are subject to us ... Truly, beyond the river of stones are the Ten Tribes of the Jews, who although they contrive kings for themselves they are in fact our servants and are tributaries to our excellency ... Before our palace stands a mirror, the ascent to which consists of five and twenty steps of porphyry and serpentine. This mirror is guarded day and night by three thousand men. We look therein and behold all that is taking place in every province and region subject to our sceptre. ...

From an Old French version of Prester John's letter (mid-13th century):

At the other side of the river that I talked about, where there are stones of such beauty, is a huge nation of Hebrews – the Ten Jewish Tribes. I know what your Jews say: that they [i.e., the Tribes] have a king who rules over their people. This is not true in the least. They are all our servants, and we receive taxes from their leader ...

Surely our men pass through the land of the great king of Israel, and his men approach our cities ... and ... buy and sell outside of our cities. For we do not want them to enter our cities nor the castles that we possess, but they may come, thanks to our permission, only to the outer limits of our cities ...

When we fight them, we take as many prisoners as we like. We kill the adults ... and ... keep the young for ourselves, so that they may serve us. Furthermore, we castrate all of them; for the men and women of this land are the most sensual people in the world and the most immodest (arrogant).

Twelfth-century Europe was mesmerized by a letter sent to the Byzantine Emperor Manuel I Komnenos by one Prester John. The latter was presumed to be a Christian monarch who reigned over a marvelous distant kingdom beyond the Arab world. Among the lands under his domain, the missive notes, are those of the Lost Tribes of Israel, whose king fits the description given by Eldad the Danite almost 300 years earlier. From this letter onwards, medieval Christians and Jews elaborated on this imaginary utopian realm. The new details and alternatives put forth over the years by the Christian and Jewish copyists-cum-editors served their respective communities' changing political, ideological, theological, and social needs.

Well known to the general public, the Prester John tradition has been the subject of extensive research.[1] The king's name debuts in a mid-twelfth-century work, *Chronica sive Historia de duabus civitatibus* (Chronicle or History of the Two Cities, 1145), as its author, Otto of Freising, shared a rumor of Prester John that he had heard from a Syrian bishop. Moreover, the first text that is attributed to this figure is the above-mentioned letter, which appeared in roughly 1165. Written in Latin, the missive describes Prester John's realm. Part of the three "Indias," this utopian kingdom is a bountiful land inhabited by a wide assortment of exotic animals and marvels, like the mythological centaurs. What is more, the king rules over dozens of other nations, and his realm borders those of the Pygmies and the legendary Amazons.

Soon after its debut, numerous versions of this letter were disseminated throughout the continent. Additionally, it was translated into almost all of the European vernacular languages as well as Hebrew. In 1177, Pope Alexander III dispatched his personal physician to find the mysterious king – a mission of which there is no further information. At the time, Prester John's realm was believed to be in Asia. However, with the discovery of the Ethiopian Christian kingdom in the thirteenth century, Europeans begin identifying it with the land of Prester John. In all likelihood, this myth was a by-product of the deteriorating fortunes of the Crusader states. Scholars have suggested that this legend echoes historical Asian figures, such as Genghis Khan or Yelü Dashi (the founder of the Qara Khitai). Other researchers have searched for clues in the sources that are alluded to in Prester John's missive: classical ethnology and mythology, Arab ethnology, and a wide array of travel literature.

With respect to the topic at hand, the letter offers the following description of the Lost Tribes: "Truly, beyond the river of stones are the ten tribes of the Jews, who although they contrive kings for themselves they are in fact our servants and are tributaries to our excellency."[2] Nineteenth- and early twentieth-century scholars assumed that the missive's writer had obtained this information from the Eldadian tradition. Abraham Epstein argued that the Prester John story was hatched for the purpose of debunking Eldad's claims of Jewish autonomy and jurisdiction.[3] What is more, David Müller juxtaposed columns of quotations from the two corpora that illustrate similarities in their content.[4]

More recently, scholars have begun to cast doubt on this seemingly obvious link between Eldad and Prester John's writing. In their edition of the Hebrew versions of the Christian monarch's letter, Edward Ullendorff and Charles Beckingham expound on this very topic. They note the parallels between the texts, like "the river of stones" and the descriptions of animals. All told, they list around twenty themes that are common to both authors.[5] Nevertheless, Ullendorff and Beckingham claim that "there are no literal resemblances so striking as to place the dependence of PJ [Prester John] on Eldad beyond any doubt."[6] In their estimation, the above-noted thesis whereby the missive was intended to falsify certain information in Eldad's oeuvre fails to explain why Prester John recycled these very narratives or why the king of the Tribes was left out of several versions of the epistle. Furthermore, they question whether it is possible that a twelfth-century Christian writer was capable of reading Hebrew. That said, many scholars, including Ullendorff and Beckingham, admit that there is no smoking gun either in support or refutation of the link between the Danite and Prester John.[7] Given the doubts concerning the provenance of Eldad's texts, David J. Wasserstein goes so far as to say that the letter might antecedent the Jewish versions of Eldad's tales.[8]

Having assayed the Eldadian literature in prior chapters, we might be more qualified to evaluate its relation to the missive under review. Some elements of the latter seem to indicate that Prester John was indeed familiar with some version of the Danite's tales. According to the monarch's letter, a river of stones descends from the high mountains where the Jews reside. Moreover, the waterway flings rocks and wood three days a week and rests for four. After a three-day journey along its banks in the direction of Prester John's realm, the river meets the "sea of sand" – a wondrous body of undulating sand that is entirely devoid of water.[9] Though it is conceivable that the author drew from other material, elements such as the Tribes' confinement behind a river that upends rocks and wood a few days a week renders the Eldad tales (or another Jewish version of this story) the most likely source.[10] Conversely, the origin of Prester John's "sea of sand" remains a question mark,[11] despite its similarity to the "river of stones." The earliest Eldad texts indeed mention that the Sambation feeds into a sea. In the context of the *sons of Moses*, these versions state that "The Holy One blessed be He has drawn a single river before them, the Sambation." To prevent anyone from reaching the sons of Moses, God not only enclosed them behind the river's banks, but saw to it that "the sea surrounds them for a distance of a three-month journey by a three-month journey."[12] At first glance, the role of this sea and its connection to the Sambation are ambiguous. Eldad appears to describe a triangular peninsula that is closed off by the sea on two sides – each of which takes ninety days to traverse – and the Sambation on the third. Like the textual revisions highlighted in chapter 2, only later versions of the tale replaced the "sea" with the "river," thereby leaving readers with the better-known image of the Tribes completely hemmed in by the Sambation. In any case, this early account[13] of the *sons of Moshe* can be considered a possible source for Prester John's "sea of sand."

Even if the missive's author refrained from copying or directly translating from Eldad, we can safely say that he was acquainted with some version – be it written or oral, unabridged or fragmentary – of the Danite's stories. Against this backdrop, the following questions beg asking: Why did Prester John decide to incorporate this particular information into his account? And how did the Jews react to this borrowing?

Let us begin with the manner in which the letter integrates material from Eldad's texts. As Epstein and others have noted, the missive presents a counter-history of the Jewish narrative:[14] "Truly, beyond the river of stones are the ten tribes of the Jews, who although they contrive kings for themselves they are in fact our servants and are tributaries to our excellency." In other words, contrary to the Jews' claims, the Tribes are *not* autonomous, but under Christian rule.

The theological underpinnings of this debate warrant a brief explanation. According to Church dogma, the Jews lost their standing as the "chosen people" to the Christians because they refused to embrace Jesus. Likewise, God's abandonment of the Jews is firmly evidenced by their loss of political power and the destruction of the Temple. In Augustine's estimation, the Jews' lack of autonomy, dispersion, and hardships substantiated the Church's triumph over Judaism. Likewise, Christians understood Jacob's blessing to Judah ("The scepter shall not depart from Judah, nor a lawgiver from between his feet, until Shiloh comes forth," Gen. 49:10) as a prophecy that the Jews' independence will cease upon the messiah's coming. As such, the Jewish people's enduring absence of a sovereign was of major Christological significance.[15] Medieval European Jewry was indeed well aware of this contention and tried to refute it. For instance, the community's speakers pointed to different interpretations of the above-cited biblical verse and to the existence of contemporaneous Jewish rulers, foremost among them the Babylonian Exilarchs.[16]

As discussed earlier, there is a consensus among scholars that the legend of the Ten Tribes' powerful kingdom and monarch served as a Jewish riposte to these sorts of claims. Although this line of defense was eschewed in the "official" Jewish–Christian disputations, the myth's reoccurrence in numerous versions of Eldad's tales speaks to the fact that the protracted dispersion of the Jewish people and its lack of autonomy had taken a psychological toll. In the coming pages, I will retrace the evolution and shifting uses of Eldad's legend within the framework of a largely hidden dialogue between Jewish and Christian society.

This chapter in the Christian–Jewish saga begins long before Eldad and his texts. In Late Antiquity, the two faiths coupled the reemergence of the Ten Tribes with the End of the Days.[17] At this early stage, Christians had yet to confer a messianic role upon the Tribes. The task of punishing the iniquitous was allotted to Gog and Magog – cruel nations that Alexander the Great reputedly cordoned off behind the Caspian Mountains.[18] In comparison to this facet of the Christian apocalypse narrative, scholars have paid less attention to the belief that the anti-Christ would emerge from the Tribe of Dan. First espoused in around the fourth century CE, this idea persisted throughout the Middle Ages.[19] Israel Yuval has demonstrated that certain messianic beliefs were shared by medieval Jews and Christians, but the two sides' interpretations sharply diverged. For example, the redemption of one party symbolized catastrophe for the other; and Jews understood the figure of the anti-Christ in their rivals' version to be no less than the Jewish Messiah.[20] Is it possible, then, that Eldad's association with the Danites was playing on an apocalyptic motif? While scholars would be hard-pressed to authoritatively settle this issue, his tales have fueled such beliefs for no less than a millennium.

As we have seen, Eldad's account depicts the Tribes as ordinary, independent nations. They are to be found in various places, just outside the borders of the known world. In all likelihood, the mere thought that the Tribes were "just around the corner" was too much for the Jewish populace to bear, as the first revision of this literature confined all them to an uncharted region of the Earth. For instance, some Hebrew versions of Eldad's tale were rewritten to correspond with older traditions whereby all of the Lost Tribes were hemmed in by the Sambation River.[21] This modification, which essentially booted the Tribes back to the realm of the imagination, perhaps suggests that this messianic phase in Jewish history had also culminated in disillusionment.

The Christian accounts have imprisoned the Ten Tribes as well. More specifically, different versions of Prester John's missive explain at length how the Israelites are prevented from leaving by a network of heavily-manned fortresses that the king installed along their borders. When necessary, Prester John also wages war against the Tribes and issues edicts barring them from entering Christian territory. All these measures are aimed at preventing the Israelites from exiting their realm, lest they destroy the world.[22] In the Latin version of the missive, "the river of stones" does not play a significant role in hindering the Tribes' movement, as the waterway runs only three days a week.[23] That said, later vernacular versions echo Jewish traditions of the river heaving up debris six days a week and resting on the Sabbath.[24]

A later Hebrew rendering of the Eldad tradition, the Constantinople print edition of 1519, betrays the influence of vernacular versions of the Prester John letter. As in the earlier Eldad tales, the sons of Moses are enclosed behind the Sambation. The text then states that "beyond the river, on the side of these three Tribes, there is a blazing fire, and no one can touch [i.e., approach, the sons of Moses] for a mile from the side of the land of the Principe."[25] Both Epstein and Müller remarked that the beginning of this passage contradicts its end, for who is on the side of the river opposite the sons of Moses – the three Tribes or "the land of the Principe"? The two scholars concluded that Principe had been interpolated by an author who was acquainted with the Prester John text.[26] From our point of view, the significance of this addition lies in the fact that the Sambation River no longer separates the Tribes from the sons of Moses. Instead, it is a barrier between the Israelites and the rest of the world.

Prester John's missive, for all its manifold incarnations, presents a consummate monarch whose impeccable conduct set a standard for Christians the world over. His efforts to prevent the Tribes from leaving their realm convey a salient message: the Jews are a threat that must be contained. The Hebrew accounts provide a foil to this narrative. More specifically, the Lost Tribes are immobilized by the Sambation, not a Christian foe. During the week, they are kept at bay by rocks and sand that the river heaves to and fro – representing nature and God's will; on the Sabbath, it is divine law and their devotion to it that stops the Israelites from crossing the border and avenging their persecutors.

While citing different reasons for this state of affairs, both Jews and Christians agree that the Tribes remain moored to their land. Only in the 1500s did a Jewish apostate to the Catholic faith challenge this narrative. In a treatise about his former co-religionists (*JudenBüchlein*), Victor von Carben (1422–1515) ironically asked why the Ten Tribes cannot cross the Sambation River on the day of rest. Jewish merchants, he noted, regularly take long trips, which span many Sabbaths. And even if they generally observe the Torah's rules, could not an exception be made for the purpose of rescuing their brethren?[27] Some Jewish versions apparently responded to this line of argumentation by introducing a new wrinkle to the story: on the Sabbath, a cloud descends over the Sambation or a fire is lit around the entire bank, either of which constitutes an insurmountable obstacle.[28]

The different versions of the Prester John letter reprise the motif of a Jewish king paying tribute to his Christian counterpart. This tax symbolizes the Lost Tribes' subordination to Prester John and the "right" order of things. In some of the texts, the levy is compensation for the resources that Prester John expends on keeping the Tribes within the limits of their realm.[29] As the Latin version already hinted, one of this corpus' objectives was to rebuff the stories that European Jews were spreading about the Lost Tribes and their monarch. This becomes evident in the vernacular versions. To the best of our knowledge, the first vernacular adaptation of Prester John was into Old French, initially as verse and then prose. Differences between this text and the Latin, such as omissions, additions, and shifts in emphasis, may reflect socio-historical developments. A case in point is these lines from the late twelfth-century French poem: "At the other side of the river that I talked about, where there are stones of such beauty, is a huge nation of Hebrews – the Ten Jewish Tribes. I know what your Jews say: that they have a king who rules over their people. This is not true in the least. They are all our servants, and we receive taxes from their leader."[30]

Viewed as authentic geographical knowledge, the Jews embraced the Prester John story, nevertheless they scrapped its Christian emphases. Abraham Abulafia's quest for the Lost Tribes, say, which was launched in 1260, opened with a search for Prester John's realm, on the premise that it indeed abutted the land of the Israelites.[31] As we have seen, the Christians also believed in the existence of the Lost Tribes. However, both communities endeavored to use these stories to their own advantage. In light of the above, there are indeed a few Hebrew translations-cum-adaptations of Prester John's missive.[32] For instance, the Jewish "editors" solved the problem of the aforementioned tribute in different ways. One Hebrew version simply jettisons this detail;[33] another short-pedals the Tribes' Jewish identity, referring to them as "not Christian," "they," "them," or "those accursed."[34] Two other versions claim that the levy was compensation for Prester John's maintenance of the shared border.[35]

In the late 1300s, Joshua of Lorca, a Spanish rabbi, wrote a letter to the Jewish apostate Pablo de Santa María (formerly Solomon ha-Levi) countering his ex-friend's arguments for embracing the Catholic faith. Disputing the claim that the Jewish people are under the yoke of Christendom, Joshua noted that only a small portion of world Jewry lives in Europe. Travelers, merchants, and books, he wrote, bear witness to the fact that there are free Jews "like those who dwell at the edge of the land of black men, which is called *al-Ḥabash* [i.e., Ethiopia]. They are neighbors of the Christian ruler named Prester John, and they sign a pact with him every year. There is no doubt about it whatsoever."[36] Put differently, Joshua replaced the one-sided tribute with a treaty between equals. This missive further demonstrates that Jews accepted the Christian version of this story, but adapted it to suit their own rhetorical needs.

With respect to the authorities' handling of the Jewish minority, the Prester John literature occasionally seems to describe the actual state of affairs in medieval Europe. In so doing, these tales justified Christian society's behavior towards its own Jewish minority. Put differently, the Prester John narrative implies that Christian society had some compunctions over the travails of the Jewish minority in its midst. For instance, a thirteenth-century French version of the epistle contains the following lines: "Surely our men pass through the land of the great king of Israel, and his men approach our cities, and they buy and sell outside of our cities. For we do not want them to enter our cities nor the castles that we possess, but they may come, thanks to our permission, only to the outer limits of our cities."[37] This passage must be understood against the backdrop of a long row of edicts banning Jews from Christian lands. In 1182, King Philippe Auguste of France temporarily expelled the Jews from his realm. Following an extensive debate, they were also deported from England in 1290. Sixteen years later, the Jewish community of northern France met a similar fate. From the latter stages of the 1200s to the end of the next century, quite a few European cities banished the Jews and restricted their commercial activity. More specifically, Jewish merchants were prohibited from conducting business within the town's walls.[38] By ascribing such behavior to Prester John, Christian authors portrayed these strictures as part of the exemplary "Christian way."

The Prester John legend was not only a window onto actual Jewish–Christian relations, but at times inverted the hierarchy. A thirteenth-century French version of the missive "chronicles" Prester John's wars with the Ten Tribes: "When we fight them, we take as many prisoners as we like. We kill the adults ... and ... keep the youth for ourselves, so that they may serve us. Furthermore, we castrate all of them, for the men and women of this land are the most sensual people in the world and the most immodest (arrogant)."[39] What are we to make of this startling excerpt? Is this struggle between imaginary Christians and Jews somehow representative of the actual relations between these groups in medieval Europe? Besides promoting the "right" order of things – that is the ascendancy of the Christians – this passage might hint at another contemporary social issue.

The peculiar motif of castration may be a reversed image of Jewish conduct towards slaves. As per Jewish law, all non-Jewish slaves working in Jewish households were required to undergo circumcision. Although this procedure was not tantamount to a conversion, it accorded them a special liminal status. The circumcision of Jewish-owned slaves in the Middle Ages is indeed a well-documented phenomenon. Time and again, this practice drew the ire of Christian neighbors, whose remonstrations often culminated in legislation outlawing this practice. Following in the footsteps of Roman (and later Byzantine) law, canonical jurisprudents viewed circumcision as not only an act of proselytism, but a form of castration.[40]

In light of the above, Prester John's emasculation of young Jewish prisoners of war perhaps constitutes a fascinating inversion. Christians apparently felt intimidated by this Jewish custom, which they evidently viewed as a breach of convention. In response to this perceived threat, they concocted a story about an exemplary Christian king that inflicted this notorious practice upon the Jews, thereby restoring the "proper" social order.

There is yet another twist to this motif. A later French version of the epistle, which is dated to roughly 1313, includes neither slaves nor castration. Instead, it adapts the earlier reference to the Jews' pre-sumed sexual character: "And know that the Jewesses are the most beautiful women in the world, and the most sensual."[41] In the first version, Jews possess a dangerous, unbridled concupiscence that must be quelled via castration. Alternatively, this French iteration depicts Jewish women as a fetching but unattainable object of Christians' sexual desire.

Generally speaking, there is a pair of contrasting medieval Christian discourses regarding Jewish sexuality: the Jews as lascivious and sexu-ally potent; and Jewish men as effeminate, namely weak, feeble, pale, and even menstruating. The first of these memes obviously portrayed Jews as a menace to Christian women and families. Oddly enough, the second played a similar role at times. During blood libels, say, the accusers contended that Jewish males "need" Christian blood because they menstruate. Through this lens, the thirteenth-century French ver-sion conveys the message that the Jews are lecherous. Therefore, they can only reside among Christians if they undergo castration. On the other hand, the early fourteenth-century adaptations of the Prester John letter exaggerate the sexuality of Jewish women. Whereas the earlier version revolves around Christian trepidation of Jews, the second emphasizes an attraction. These differences notwithstanding, both of these feelings pertain to sex and are articulated in a bold manner. For instance, the enchanting Jewesses are portrayed as "arrogant" – a trait that necessitates their "submission" or "conquest." Maybe the expulsion of the Jews from Northern France at 1306 by Philippe le Bel that derived, among other reasons, from vast popular anti-Semitic sentiments, is represented by the version portraying fear of the Jews to a point that demands their "castration." This expulsion was followed by a sense of nostalgia and need for the Jews – a need that was fulfilled with their temporary return at 1315, called by Louis X le Hutin.[42] This may provide a possible background, among others, for the version depicting longing for Jewish women, written around 1313.

In response to these Christian aspersions, did Jews invoke Eldad for the purpose of substantiating their tradition of the Lost Tribes? This sort of use turns up in a Christian work, of all things, *The Travels of Sir John of Mandeville*. Fusing information from Prester John with other material, such as ethnographic writing, *Mandeville's Travels* was, according to most scholars, originally written in around 1366 by a priest in a Norman-French dialect (though an English provenance cannot be ruled out). Mandeville's imaginary itinerary blends genuine travel accounts with imaginary descriptions, which were culled from a farrago of sources.[43] Aside for reproducing a version of Prester John's letter, the book tells of Jewish Tribes that were confined between the Caspian Mountains by its rugged terrain and a few other insurmountable obstacles. Nonetheless,

> If they were to leave by that sea, they wouldn't know where to disembark as they understand no language except their own ... Sometimes it has happened that a few of the Jews have made it over the hills, but a large number of people could not travel over these mountains, they are so huge and high.[44]

This account reflects the Christian belief that someone has actually managed to "escape" from the realm of the Tribes. Moreover, it alludes to one of Eldad's special characteristics: Hebrew monolingualism. This element, which for Jews is an exotic attestation of Eldad's Danite origins, is construed by Christians as another chain in the Israelites' shackles.

This transition from the fantastic (the land of the Tribes) to the real (Europe) is bridged by shared knowledge of Hebrew. More specifically, John of Mandeville concludes his fictional description by uniting the mythical Lost Tribes with their brethren in Europe:

People of the neighboring region say that in the era of Antichrist these Jews will do much harm to Christians. Therefore all the Jews who live in other parts of the world have learned to speak Hebrew, because they believe that the Jews living amongst the mountains will emerge and speak nothing but Hebrew. Then the other Jews will speak Hebrew to them and lead them into Christendom in order to ravage the Christians.[45]

In fact, many Christian texts also describe the Jews as waiting for the Lost Tribes to rescue them from their adversaries. Dated to roughly 1330, one German apocalyptic text even claimed that there are Christians who revere the Tribes: "Jews and many Judaizing Christians imagine that this people is holy: they would be glad if they were to come and would join them at once."[46] This unique embracement of a Jewish tradition should not be taken at face value, for it is most likely a by-product of this work's special character – a treatise against the Waldensian heresy.

Surprisingly enough, a thirteenth-century Jewish source, *Sefer ha-Maskil* (The Book of the Erudite), contains a similar messianic internalization. Contrary to the prevailing Jewish stance, its author, Solomon ben Eliezer, unequivocally affirms the Christian view that the Ten Tribes are subordinate to Prester John: "And why was [wicked][47] Edom [i.e., Christianity] fortunate enough to have more Jews subject to it than to all the other nations, to the point where they are even subject to the kingdom of Prester John, who is from Edom?"[48] The answer, which is not germane to the topic at hand, refers to Isaac's blessing of Esau – the father of biblical Edom. That said, a Jewish offshoot of this discourse warrants our undivided attention. Taking advantage of this Christian perspective on Isaac's prophecy, Solomon ben Eliezer calculated that while commencing in 1296, the messianic process will only come to fruition in 1405. Moreover, he believes that the Jews must suffer before they are redeemed. In Solomon ben Eliezer's view, they will only be completely liberated from the Diaspora if they endure severe and protracted oppression at the hands of the nations. For this reason, he readily accepted the Christian myth of the Tribes' subjugation under Prester John, for it is evidence that the messiah is near. Put differently, the Christians' haughty preponderance foreshadows their imminent downfall, in fulfillment of the divine plan. Solomon even put a positive spin on the Exile's protracted duration. Drawing on Psalm 90:15, he contended that the messianic age will last as long as the Jewish Exile: "Give us joy for as long as Thou hast afflicted us, for as long as the years we have suffered misfortune" (Psalm 90:15).[49]

From the distance of time, Solomon's interpretation appears to be a passive psychological mechanism for coping with the harshness of the Jewish existence in Christian lands. However, this reading was not understood in this manner during the Middle Ages. A generation later, John of Mandeville concluded his account of the Lost Tribes' internment behind the Caspian Gates thus:

> these [i.e., European] Jews says that they know through their prophecies that the Jews who are within these Caspian Mountains will emerge and Christians will be subjected to them as they have been subjected to Christians.[50]

In other words, Christians saw this Jewish belief not as a passive projection into the far future, but as a vigorous attempt on the part of European Jewry to exact revenge. How this Jewish apocalyptic hope reached Christian ears is unknown. Perhaps this information found its way to the majority society through converts or inter-faith dialogues, like the public disputations. In any case, Christians were undoubtedly familiar with this belligerent Jewish prophecy.

Christian society's acquaintance with the inner thoughts of the oppressed Jewish minority had actual implications. Scholars have shown that during the twelfth century, when the legend of Prester John first began to spread, Christians took to identifying the Lost Tribes with Gog and Magog and the barbaric nations that Alexander the Great enclosed behind the Caspian Gates.[51] Often intermingled, these two legends depict the horrors of the apocalypse and human cruelty. What is more, they delineate the limits of the humanity.[52] The association of the Jews with these nations, as well as the devil, in the era's Christian discourse was part and parcel of a dehumanization campaign against Jewish society. In a similar vein, the Jews were accused of being irrational.[53] This, then, might explain why the Mongols were identified with the Ten Tribes as the Khan's forces were drawing ever closer to Europe in the 1240s.[54] Given the hopes that they placed on their lost brethren, it comes as no surprise that European Jewry also embraced this affiliation with the Asian nomads. Whereas the Christians viewed the Mongols as a destructive juggernaut, in Jewish eyes the approaching horde could be seen as a potential savior.[55]

During these years, Meshullam de Piera, a Jewish Spaniard, composed a poem expressing the wish that the Ten Tribes will liberate their co-religionists from their pitiable existence and punish the Christians. Meshullam even mentions "the rumor that our enclosed brothers are coming." In addition, his poem interspersed themes from the Eldad corpus along with legends of Prester John, Gog and Magog, and Alexander the Great.[56]

A later Hebrew source, in all likelihood from early fifteenth-century Sicily, recounts an apocalyptic frenzy that was triggered by rumors that the "enclosed ones" had arrived. This fragmentary letter, which was preserved in the Cairo Geniza, contains the following news:

> Your secreted king [i.e., the monarch of the Ten Tribes] dispatched missives to the king of Spain, the king of Germany, and to all those kingdoms, and they are formulated [thus]: "I order you ... to give assistance to my envoys so that they may go to all the communi[ties] of Israel [and deliver this message:] All of you shall assemble for the sake of going to Jerusal[em]." The kin[g]s will not be able to prevent them ... The king of Spain, the king of Germany, the king of Hungary, and the king of France are terrified and quaking. Hence, they are rounding up a great deal of money and a formidable army. Should the enclosed ones agree to take the money, [then all the better]; and if not, they will confront them [i.e., the Lost Tribes, on the battle pitch].[57]

This text demonstrates how Jews enlisted the image of the Ten Tribes. Besides announcing the Tribes' imminent arrival, the author included a stern warning: "If they [i.e., the Tribes] come and hear that they [Christians] killed the Jews, they will kill you [the Christians they encounter] in their place."

In the absence of any true political power, the Jews inverted their lowly existence into an imagined, glorious kingdom populated by their lost brethren who possess all the trappings of independence that the former lacked. Thereafter, the Diaspora wielded the myth of the Ten Tribes as a cudgel: if the Christians refuse to stop persecuting the Jews, this weapon would be put to use. This image was indeed projected back onto reality, as European Jewry was cast in the image of the mighty Israelites. For example, the chronicle of Matthew Paris, a thirteenth-century English monk, indicates that this message found a captive audience in Christian society.[58] Amid the Mongol advance to Central Europe in 1241, Jews in Germany believed that the Asian warriors might be the Ten Tribes coming to their rescue. What is more, several Jews were accused of collaborating with the Mongols.[59] In the trial, according to Paris, the Jewish defendants claimed that they were equipping the hordes with poisoned provisions. However, investigators revealed that they were indeed selling the Khan undamaged goods, including arms. Consequently, many Jews were executed for aiding the enemy.

This episode speaks to the potentially tragic outcome of inter-
mingling fact with fiction. Owing to false portrayals of Jewish might,
Christian society misconstrued itself as weak and, in a putative act of
defense, assailed the helpless Jews in their midst.

In summation, both Jews and Christians alike believed in the existence
of Prester John's kingdom and the neighboring Lost Tribes. The two
societies exchanged information about these legendary realms, elaborat-
ing on and integrating the other's versions into their own. The mere fact
that they shared this knowledge only burnished the credibility of these
tales. What is more, these commonly-held myths served as a battlefield
upon which Europe's Jews and Christians fought an all-too-real campaign. As is often the case with stories of fantastical places, this one
reinforced the existing social order in which Christians reigned over Jews,
and both sides accepted, explained, and rationalized this state of affairs.

Nevertheless, there were also instances in which this hierarchy was
called into question. In consequence, far-off apocalyptic scenarios sud-
denly appeared to be imminent. Eldad freed the Ten Tribes from their
imagined captivity beyond the Sambation into the real world. Though
both Jews and Christians sought to re-confine the Israelites to the realm
of legend, the stories occasionally had a tangible effect on inter-faith
relations in Europe. At times of strife, the Jews brandished these mythical
figures as a threat in the hopes of persuading Christian society to forego
its discriminatory ways, exploiting their rivals' deepest fears. On occasion,
though, these steps backfired on the Jewish community, as Christians
actually identified this minority group with the powerful Lost Tribes. For
the sake of defending themselves against this chimera, they assaulted the
real, yet powerless, Jews in the immediate vicinity.

Notes

1 I availed myself of the following versions of the Prester John letter: Frie-
   drich Zarncke, *Der Priester Johannes*, 2 vols. (Leipzig 1876–1879); Bettina
   Wagner, *Die 'Epistola presbiteri Johannis' lateinisch und deutsch: Überlie-
   ferung, Textgeschichte, Rezeption und Übertragungen im Mittelalter*
   (Tübingen 2000); Charles F. Beckingham and Bernard Hamilton, eds.,
   Prester John, the Mongols and the Ten Lost Tribes (Aldershot, Hampshire:
   Variorum, 1996), 40–102; Martin Gosman, *La lettre du Prêtre Jean: les
   versions en ancien français et en ancien occitan, textes et commentaires*
   (Groningen 1982). A new edition and translation was recently published
   by: Keagen Brewer, *Prester John: The Legend and its Sources, Crusade
   Texts in Translation*, vol. 27 (Ashgate 2015). The literature on this figure is
   copious. In addition to the above-cited editions, here is a partial list of
   notable works on this topic: Charles E. Nowell, "The Historical Prester
   John," *Speculum* 28/3 (1953): 435–445; Charles F. Beckingham, "The

72   *Jews and Christians*

Achievements of Prester John," in *Prester John, the Mongols and the Ten Lost Tribes*, 1–24; Ulrich Knefelkamp, "Der Priesterkönig Johannes und sein Reich – Legende oder Realität," *Journal of Medieval History* 14 (1988): 337–355; István Bejczy, *La lettre du Prêtre Jean: une utopie médiévale* (Paris 2001); Manuel João Ramos, *Essays in Christian Mythology: The Metamorphosis of Prester John* (New York, Toronto, and Oxford 2006).

2 Brewer, *Prester John*, 76; Zarncke, *Der Priester Johannes*, 915, # 41; Wagner, *Die 'Epistola presbiteri Johannis'*, 361, # 41.

3 Epstein, 15.

4 Müller, 4–8.

5 Edward Ullendorff and Charles F. Beckingham, *The Hebrew Letters of Prester John* (Oxford 1982), 153–172.

6 Ibid., 156.

7 Ibid., 155–159. For similar assessments: Bernard Hamilton, "Prester John and the Three Kings of Cologne," in Henry Mayr-Harting and Robert Ian Moore, eds., *Studies in Medieval History Presented to R. H. C. Davis* (London 1985), 185; Abraham Gross, "The Expulsion and the Search for the Ten Tribes," *Judaism* 41/2 (1992): 132; Andrew C. Gow, *The Red Jews: Antisemitism in an Apocalyptic Age 1200–1600, Studies in Medieval and Reformation Thought*, vol. LV (Leiden 1995), 40–41; *inter alia*.

8 David J. Wasserstein, "Eldad ha-Dani and Prester John," in *Prester John, the Mongols and the Ten Lost Tribes*, 213–236. Krauss had the insight to claim that some parts of the Eldad corpus are earlier to the Prester John texts while others are later and echo that legend – similar to what I claim below – like Wasserstein he called for a philological study of Eldad's texts in order to judge the question. See: Krauss, "New Light on Geographical Information of Eldad Hadani and Benjamin of Tudela."

9 Zarncke, *Der Priester Johannes*, 914–915; Wagner, *Die 'Epistola presbiteri Johannis'*, 352–353.

10 That said, the River Sambation turns up in early works. See: Kokin, "Toward the Source of the Sambatyon."

11 John L. Lowes, "The Dry Sea and the Carrenare," *Modern Philology* 3/1 (1905): 9–19; Knefelkamp, "Der Priesterkönig Johannes und sein Reich," 344; *Carta do Preste João das Índias: Versões medievais latinas*, trans. L. Buescu (Lisbon 1998), 131, § 31.

12 Epstein, 65; Müller, 63.

13 E.g., Mss. Roma - Biblioteca Casanatense, 3097. For a fuller philological discussion see: Micha J. Perry, "The Imaginary War between Prester John and Eldad the Danite and Its Real Implications," *Viator* 41/1 (2010): 5–10.

14 In using the term "counter-history," I follow in the footsteps of Amos Funkenstein, *Perceptions of Jewish History* (Berkeley 1993), 22–49.

15 Jeremy Cohen, *Living Letters of the Law: Ideas of the Jew in Medieval Christianity* (Berkeley 1999), 30–35.

16 For instance, the Jewish polemicists cited from the *Babylonian Talmud*, Sanhedrin, 5a.

17 Robert L. Bensly, *The Fourth Book of Ezra* (Nendeln, Liechtenstein Reprint, 1967), chapter 13, 40–46; *Commodiani Carmina, Instructionum*, liber II, Cap. I, *Corpus Scriptorum Ecclesiasticorum Latinorum*, v. 15 (1887), 57–67; *Jerusalem Talmud*, Sanhedrin, chapter 10, no. 5, p. 53b.

18 Andrew R. Anderson, *Alexander's Gate, Gog and Magog, and the Inclosed Nations*, Monographs of the Medieval Academy of America, no. 5 (Cambridge, MA 1932), 58–86.

19 Jeremy Cohen, "Antichrist and His Jewish Connections," *Rishonim ve-Achronim: Studies in Jewish History Presented to Avraham Grossman* (Jerusalem 2010), 29–45.

20 Israel Jacob Yuval, *Two Nations in Your Womb: Perceptions of Jews and Christians in Late Antiquity and the Middle Ages*, trans. Barbara Harshav and Jonathan Chipman (Berkeley 2006), 288–289.

21 A case in point is a responsum by R. Nissim of Qayrawān: Epstein, 101; *Yalkut Shim'oni*, Isaiah, no. 469 [Hebrew]; Nachmanides, Bible Exegesis on Deuteronomy 32:26 [Hebrew].

22 See, for instance: Wagner, *Die 'Epistola presbiteri Johannis'*, 391, lns. 143–154, lns. 438–439; Gosman, *La lettre du Prêtre Jean*, 196–199, 342–345, lns. 218.2–227.

23 Zarncke, *Der Priester Johannes*, 914, no. 33; Wagner, *Die 'Epistola presbiteri Johannis'*, 358, 360, 375, 439–440.

24 Gosman, *La lettre du Prêtre Jean*, 194–197, 341–343; 462–463, lns. 217–218. See as well: Zarncke, *Der Priester Johannes*, 952, ln. 11; Gow, *The Red Jews*, 309.

25 Epstein, 55; Müller, 68, B, 19g.

26 Epstein, 63, n. 29; Müller, 25; Ullendorff and Beckingham, *The Hebrew Letters of Prester John*, 25–26, 70, n. 1.

27 Cited in Gow, *The Red Jews*, 247–252.

28 Epstein, 39, 55, 65; Müller, 68–69.

29 For example: Wagner, *Die 'Epistola presbiteri Johannis'*, 391. Other examples of this sort of interpretation can be found in Gosman, *La lettre du Prêtre Jean*, 198–199, 344–345, lns. 228–232.

30 Gosman, *La lettre du Prêtre Jean*, 122. Fourteenth-century German versions: Zarncke, *Der Priester Johannes*, 963, lns. 538–583; Gow, *The Red Jews*, 311; Wagner, *Die 'Epistola presbiteri Johannis'*, 524–547.

31 Adolph Jellinek, *Bet ha-Midrasch; Sammlung Kleiner Midraschim*, vol. III (Leipzig 1853), XLII.

32 Ullendorff and Beckingham, *The Hebrew Letters of Prester John*. For more insight on these letters, see Kenneth R. Stow, "Reviewed Work: *The Hebrew Letters of Prester John* by Edward Ullendorff and Charles F. Beckingham," *Speculum* 59 (1984): 447–449; Norman Roth "Review of *The Hebrew Letters of Prester John,* eds. Edward Ullendorff and C. F. Beckingham," *Hebrew Studies* 25 (1984): 192–195; Steven Kaplan, "A Note on the Hebrew Letters of Prester John," *Journal of Jewish Studies* 36/2 (1985): 230–234.

33 Ullendorff and Beckingham, ibid., 57–61. This text is from Mss. NY JTS Rab. 34 (Adler 2237), fol. 231–238b. On its dating see: Perry, "The Imaginary War," 14, n. 57.

34 Ullendorff and Beckingham, ibid., 132–133.

35 Ibid., 97, 148–149.

36 Judah D. Eisenstein, *Ozar Wikuhim: A Collection of Polemics and Disputations* (New York 1928), 99.

37 Gosman, *La lettre du Prêtre Jean*, 349–351, Ms. M, lns. 245.1–248.1.

38 Baron, *A Social and Religious History of the Jews*, 271–280.

39 Gosman, *La lettre du Prêtre Jean*, 351–353, Ms. M, lns. 248.1–253.
40 Solomon Grayzel, *The Church and the Jews in the XIIIth Century*, vol. 2: "1254–1314," ed. Kenneth R. Stow (New York 1989), 246–247; Shlomo Simonson, *The Apostolic See and the Jews*, vol. VII: History (Toronto 1991), 159; Amnon Linder, *The Jews in the Legal Sources of the Early Middle Ages* (Detroit 1997), index, s.v. "Jews: Circumcision"; idem, *The Jews in Roman Imperial Legislation* (Detroit and Jerusalem 1987), nos. 1, 6, 10, 11, 44, 48, 54.
41 Gosman, *La lettre du Prêtre Jean*, 468, Mss. WXY, lns. 252–253. These manuscripts are explicated in ibid., 34, 86–90.
42 On the expulsion see: William Chester Jordan, *The French Monarchy and the Jews: From Philip Augustus to the Last Capetians* (Philadelphia 1989), 177–248.
43 On Mandeville, see the introduction in: Anthony Bale, *The Book of Marvels and Travels* (Oxford 2012).
44 Ibid., 105.
45 Ibid. On Hebrew texts as a threat to Christians, see Ruth Nisse, "A Romance of the Jewish East: The Ten Lost Tribes and The Testaments of the Twelve Patriarchs in Medieval Europe," *Medieval Encounters* 13 (2007): 499–523.
46 The Passau Anonymous (c. 1330), cited from Gow, *The Red Jews*, 205–206 (German text), 207 (English translation). Alexander Patschovsky offers an in-depth look of this work; idem, *Der Passauer Anonymus: Ein Sammelwerk über Ketzer, Juden, Antichrist aus der Mitte des 13. Jahrhunderts* (Stuttgart 1968).
47 At this point in the text, a word—most likely "wicked"—was expunged by a Christian censor.
48 *Sefer ha-Maskil* has never been brought to print. The only extant version is in manuscript form: Ms. Moscow - Russian State Library, Ms. Guenzburg 508, fol. 37a.
49 This verse was already used to calculate the duration of the messianic era in the Talmud (b. Sanhedrin, 99a). The equation "length of suffering/exile = time of rejoicing/messiah" was widespread among European Jews in the early Middle Ages. See, for example, Solomon Buber, *Midrash on Psalm, also known as Shocher Tov* (1891), chapter 90, p. 17 [Hebrew]; Rashi Commentary on the Bible, Psalm 90:15 [Hebrew]; Elazar ben Judah of Worms, *The Commentary on the Prayer Book of the Rokheach*, ed. Moshe Hershler and Yehudah Alter Hershler (Jerusalem 1992), 96 [Hebrew].
50 Bale, *The Book of Marvels and Travels*, 105. Christians were acquainted with similar Jewish ideas before Mandeville's time. For instance: *Matthew Paris's English History: From the Year 1235 to 1273*, trans. John A. Giles (London 1852), 357.
51 Anderson, *Alexander's Gate*, 58–86; Gow, *The Red Jews*, 42–48.
52 Daniel Baraz, *Medieval Cruelty: Changing Perceptions, Late Antiquity to the Early Modern Period* (Ithaca 2003), 75–105.
53 Robert Bonfil, "The Devil and the Jews in the Christian Consciousness of the Middle Ages," in Shmuel Almog, ed., *Antisemitism through the Ages* (Oxford 1988), 91–98; Cohen, *Living Letters of the Law*, 313–364.
54 Felicitas Schmieder, "Christians, Jews, Muslims – and Mongols: Fitting a Foreign People into the Western Christian Apocalyptic Scenario," *Medieval Encounters* 12/2 (2006): 274–295.

55 Yuval, *Two Nations in Your Womb*, 257–295. For the most part, my analysis follows in Yuval's footsteps.

56 Jefim (Haim) Schirmann, *Hebrew Poetry in Spain and Provençe*, vol. 2 (Jerusalem 1961), 317 [Hebrew]; Tova Rosen, "Kazahrs, Mongols, and the Pains of the Time of *Messiah*," in Michal Oron, ed., *Between History and Literature* (Tel Aviv 1983), 42–59 [Hebrew].

57 Ms. T.S. Misc. 35.16. Published in Jacob Mann, *Text and Studies in Jewish History and Literature*, vol. I (Cincinnati 1931), 34–44; Nadia Zaldes, "A Magical Event in Sicily: Notes and Clarifications on the Messianic Movement in Sicily," *Zion* 58/3 (1993): 347–363 [Hebrew].

58 *Matthew Paris's English History*, 357–358. See Sophia Menache, "Matthew Paris's Attitudes Toward Anglo-Jewry," *Journal of Medieval History* 23/2 (1997): 139–162.

59 Sophia Menache, "Tartars, Jews, Saracens and the Jewish-Mongol 'Plot' of 1241," *History* 81 (1996): 319–342; Israel J. Yuval, "Jewish Messianic Expectations towards 1240 and Christian Reactions," in Peter Schäfer and Mark Cohen, eds., *Toward the Millennium –Messianic Expectations from the Bible to Waco* (Leiden 1998), 105–121. On the Lost Tribes (who are referred to as the "Red Jews" in the German tradition) after the fourteenth century, see Rebekka Voß, *Umstrittene Erlöser. Politik, Ideologie und jüdisch-christlicher Messianismus in Deutschland, 1500–1600* (Göttingen 2011), 92–122.

8   Black and white

Responsa of David ben Solomon ben Zimra (1479–1573, Egypt):

Question:
There was a case involving a Kushite woman from the Land of
Kush named Alḥabash, who was taken captive along with her two
sons, whereupon she was purchased by [an Egyptian Jew] Reuben.
We asked her what her background is. And she said that she was
married and these are her sons from her husband, who is called so-
and-so and this son of mine his name is so-and-so. Enemies came
upon them and killed all the men that were in the synagogue,[1] they
were plundered and the woman and children were taken captive. It
turns out that she is from the seed of Israel, from the tribe of Dan
that dwells in the Kush Mountains. From then on, they [i.e., the
local community] have held her to be an *agunah* [literally "anchored
woman," a wife whose husband has gone missing]. Sometime later,
her master Reuben had relations with her and begot a son. And he
[the boy] grew up and indeed wants to take a wife from among the
Jewish community and be part of it. You have asked of me if he is
worthy of entering the community and can we amend his status?

Answer:
… All the more so, I say that even according to her words, she is
presumed to be a married woman, for it is widely known that there
is an eternal war between the kings of Kush, which consists of
three kingdoms – some of them Ishmaelites and some of them
Arameans who hold to their faith, and some of them are Israelites
from the tribe of Dan … as far as can be seen, they are from the
sect of Zadok and Boethus who are referred to as Karaites, for
they do not know the oral law and do not light candles on Sabbath
eve. And the war between them [i.e., the kingdoms] does not cease,

and prisoners are taken from both sides every day. Hence, she could not have claimed [there is] "peace in the world," as it is known that there is no peace there [in Kush].

What is more, there is an overriding rule concerning the Karaites, as it is evident that they are Jews. Their marriage ceremonies are binding, [but] their divorces are not in line with the regulation of our sages of blessed memory. In addition, they are all disqualified according to the Bible from giving testimony. Owing to the grave danger latent in this query, for several of their families have entered the Jewish community, I did not see [fit] to expand on this, and it is best that they be [considered] unintentional [sinners, than intentional sinners]. In any event, I admit that if all of them were to agree to enter the religion of the fellowship [i.e., rabbinic Judaism], take upon themselves the traditions of our rabbis of blessed memory, to be like us, I would allow them to enter the community with the sages' approval ... I would not be worried about this to the point of removing the name of the [Jewish] nation [from the ranks of Ethiopian Jewry], for it is a far-fetched concern ... This is the ruling on these matters: since the prohibition has not been clarified, if they would agree to return to us and accept the terms of the fellowship, it would be like breaking off a chip from a log for all my colleagues [i.e., it would be easy for the halakhic authorities to find consensus] to allowed them to enter the community. (*Responsa of David Ben Zimra*, part IV, clause 119)

Question:
You asked of me to inform you of my opinion regarding one that bought a freed slave from those same Jews residing in the Land of Kush. How should he [i.e., the master] conduct himself with him [the slave]. Should he be released in six [years, as a Hebrew slave] or not? And do all the laws that apply to [Jewish] slaves pertain to him or not?

Answer:
... Hence, the one who bought the free slave, since it turned out that he is Jewish, this is indeed [a case of] redemption of captives, not the purchase of slaves. The commandment to ransom him, lest he become assimilated among the nations, falls on all the Jewish people. More so this one ... the entire Jewish people are commanded to ransom him, and he who bought him [i.e., the captured Jew] first merited [to perform] a great deed. At any rate, he does not have the legal classification of a slave ... Be that as it may, there is another doubt, for all those Ḥabesha [i.e., Abyssinians] residing in the Land of Kush conduct themselves like [members of]

the Karaite faith, who are [equated with] Zadok and Boethus. And are we not commanded to refrain from either redeeming or resuscitating them? In any event, I infer from these words that those who live amid the rabbis and see [*sic*] the teachings of the sages and denigrate and scorn them, it is of these and their ilk that [the sages] said: We lower and do not elevate [them out of a ditch during the Sabbath]. As Maimonides of blessed memory wrote, they are the accursed family. However, those who come from the Land of Kush are undoubtedly from the tribe of Dan. Since none of their sages possessed the [oral] tradition, they held only the literal [interpretation] of the writ. But if they would have been taught [the oral law], they would not have denied the words of our rabbis of blessed memory. And they are akin to "children who were taken captive by the nations [=sinners by dint of ignorance]." [You should] know that Zadok and Boethus were indeed in the second Temple and the tribe of Dan was deported beforehand. And even if you are inclined to say that it is doubtful nevertheless it is a commandment to ransom them. (*Responsa of David Ben Zimra*, part VII, Laws of Agunot, clause 5)

R. Ovadia Yosef's letter from 1973:

Therefore, I have come to the conclusion that the Falasha are the descendants of the tribes of Israel that travelled south to Kush, and there is no doubt that the above-mentioned *geonim* [=great rabbis] who established that they are from the tribe of Dan researched, interpreted, and came to this conclusion in accordance with the most reliable testimonies and evidence. I too, the youngest among all of the tribes of Israel, diligently researched and interpreted their affairs after the leaders of the Falasha turned to me with the request to join our brethren, the house of Israel, in the spirit of the Torah and Halakha, the written and oral Torah, without any reservations, and to observe the commandments of the holy Torah, as per the dictates of our rabbis of blessed memory from whose words we live. And I decided that to the best of my knowledge, the Falasha are Jews and that we must save them from absorption and assimilation, must expedite their immigration to the Land [of Israel], educate them in the spirit of our holy Torah, and involve them in the building of our sacred land. And may the sons return to their borders. (*Yabia omer*, part VIII, § 1)

To this point, we have tracked Eldad the Danite's long and winding road to acceptance in the Jewish world. Along the way, his corpus was transformed from a dubious and problematic source to one that is on par with the rest of the Jewish bodies of knowledge. Among the milestones in this process was R. Zemaḥ, the Babylonian gaon, integrating Eldad's "Talmud" into, or even subordinated it into, his own system of knowledge (chapter 3); copyists adapting his bizarre legal traditions to suit the Babylonian Talmud (chapter 4); and the ultimate acceptance of his unconventional views on the place of women as a worthy "custom" and "stricture" (chapter 6). The present chapter will explain how Eldad constitutes the "given" that cleared away the doubts as to the Beta-Israel's Jewishness. More specifically, the ancient information about this figure was the element that enabled the Jewish world to absorb Ethiopian Jewry's foreignness between the sixteenth and twentieth centuries. As researchers have shown, the Beta-Israel were identified with the tribe of Dan and Eldad in an instinctive (or labored) manner.[2] What is more, in my estimation, Eldad's so-called "Talmud," his traditions that were crafted in the aftermath of the Temple's destruction, came to be associated with Ethiopian Jewry. This association indeed qualified them as authentic Jews or, alternatively, constituted a stumbling block to their absorption into orthodox Judaism and Israeli society. Let us open, then, with a survey of Ethiopian Jewish history. This will be followed by an in-depth look at mainstream Jewry's identification of this group with Eldad the Danite and the ramifications thereof.

Ethiopia was among the first kingdoms to officially adopt the Christian faith. The religious literature in the Ge'ez (ancient Ethiopic) language, which over the centuries preserved ancient books and traditions that the Occident had lost, bears witness to Ethiopian contacts with early Christians, who introduced the Bible to the kingdom. According to scholars, a group possessing Jewish identity existed as a distinct tribe in Ethiopia from as far back as the fourth century. In parallel to Ethiopia's Christianization (and perhaps as a reaction against this turn of events), this community appears to have embraced a Jewish identity, and especially the Old Testament. With the passage of time, the tribe came to be known as Beta-Israel or the Falashas, i.e., "stranger" or "wanderer," in Amharic – a derogatory term that was coined by the group's enemies. Steven Kaplan posits that its Jewish identity slowly evolved between the 1300s and 1500s.[3] The first to hear about the Beta-Israel's lore from the actual members were nineteenth-century travelers to the Horn of Africa. By virtue of their accounts, we know that the Beta-Israel considered themselves the progeny of King Solomon and Queen Sheba. This myth is analogous to that of the

Ethiopian royal family according to which Emperor Menelik I is a descendant of these same Biblical figures. In addition, Ethiopian chronicles mention that it fought a Jewish tribe led by one Queen Zewditu (i.e., Judith) in the Middle Ages.

Beta-Israel was indeed a recognized group within Ethiopia's tribal mix at the outset of the modern era. Maintaining its own settlements, this group also stood out for the vocations that its members specialized in, particularly weaving, blacksmithing, and construction. Later sources seem to imply that the Beta-Israel practiced a Biblical faith: extreme Sabbath observance; rigid isolation of menstrual women; dietary kashrut, and scriptural festivals celebrated with long prayer services constituted of Bible readings, and sacrifices. Furthermore, they kept laws of purity and segregation *vis-à-vis* other religious groups and developed a strong and distinctive Jewish self-consciousness.

In turn, neighboring tribes devised superstitions that scapegoated the Beta-Israel for every disaster or trouble to strike the region. For instance, it was believed that at night Beta-Israel turned into *bouda* – a sort of demon (or hyena) that killed people, burnt down huts and villages, and spread virulent disease. As revenge for ostensibly igniting these calamities, they were murdered on a somewhat regular basis. Over the generations, Christians sought to forcibly convert the Beta-Israel. Non-Jewish sources even relate incidents where members resisted Christianization, much like Jewish martyrs in Europe and beyond, at the cost of their lives. Throughout the 1800s, attempts to convert the Beta-Israel proliferated, despite (and perhaps because of) the Jewish world's efforts to intervene on their behalf. For instance, Swedish and English Protestant missions to Ethiopia (both of whom were expelled from the monarchy at a certain stage) trained local devotees to convert Beta-Israel. These initiatives lassoed in a fair share of new recruits.

These forms of adversity took their toll on Ethiopian Jewry. For generations, the Beta-Israel had held on to the belief that the messiah would come and usher in the End of the Days. However, by the nineteenth century, they had lost hope that this prophecy would be fulfilled.

At this crucial juncture, an Orthodox Polish Jew and Orientalist by the name of Jacques Faitlovitch (1888–1951) breathed new life into Ethiopian Jewry. Though hardly the first Jewish writer to occupy himself or meet with the Beta-Israel, he was the one that forged a lasting bond between this group and world Jewry.[4] After familiarizing himself with the Ethiopian language, culture, and literature, Faitlovitch visited the Beta-Israel on several occasions. Propelling mainstream Judaism into action, the Orientalist brought Beta-Israel youth to Jerusalem and Europe for schooling. Thereafter, he even founded a Jewish school in

Eritrea where the youth returning from abroad served as teachers. This enterprise pushed the community into the arms of Rabbinic Jewry. From that point forward, the religio-cultural gap between the Beta-Israel and the Jewish world was gradually closed. Faitlovitch's efforts would culminate with Operation Moses – the State of Israel's campaign to bring Ethiopian Jewry back to Zion in 1984 (followed with Operation Solomon in 1991).

It bears noting that the vast majority of contemporary accounts of the ties with the Beta-Israel open with Eldad the Danite. Towards the end of the Middle Ages, Prester John was widely identified with Ethiopia, which was indeed the largest Christian kingdom in Africa. As we have seen, the Jews also believed in the existence of Prester John. Similarly, Jewish writers identified Ethiopia as the domain of the Lost Tribes from as early as the 1400s, when the first rumors about this tribe/kingdom reached mainstream Jewry. This outlook comes to expression in letters on this topic by Jerusalem-based rabbis as well as R. Elijah of Ferrara and R. Ovadiah Bertinoro.[5] Unlike their predecessors, the authors of these same epistles were spurred on by direct encounters with "Abyssinian Jews." Faithful to the spirit of their age, early modern explorers searched high and low for the lost Israelites in the foreign lands that had recently opened up to European society. Against this backdrop, the said reports from the Horn of Africa had a strong air of verisimilitude.

In the sixteenth century, David ben Solomon ben Zimra, a Spanish-born rabbi known by the acronym RaDBaZ, met Habesha Jews in Egypt. There are indeed a number of references to Ethiopian Jewry in the writing of ben Zimra, who presided over the Egyptian Jewish community. Most notably, he responds to a pair of questions concerning the Beta-Israel's Jewishness. The first is the riveting case of "a Kushite woman" who was apparently purchased by an Egyptian Jew in a slave market.[6] According to the woman's testimony, her husband had been killed by "enemies," while she and her two boys were kidnapped and sold. "It turns out," according to text of the query, "that she is from the seed of Israel, from the tribe of Dan dwelling in the Kush Mountains." This passive language ("It turns out") perhaps indicates that the slave did not tell the Egyptian Jews about her Danite origin, but the details thereof were inferred from her revelation that she is, say, a Jew or member of the Beta-Israel. In any event, the conclusion that she is from the tribe of Dan is essential, for there is a major difference between viewing the Beta-Israel as progeny of the Danites who were believed to have left the kingdom of Israel shortly before the first Temple was destroyed or as scion of King Solomon and Queen Sheba or exiles who reached the Horn of Africa after the destruction of the second Temple.

At any rate, the question that was submitted to ben Zimra centers around the remainder of this incident. The slave's master – a Jew by the name of Reuben – begot a son from her, and it was uncertain as to whether the boy fell under the heading of a *mamzer* (Hebrew for "bastard", i.e., according to Biblical law a child who was born to a married woman from someone other than her husband). From a religio-legal point of view, the crux of the matter is whether the woman is an *agunah* (a married woman whose husband is missing). Put differently, was she still married upon bearing this child? If so, he is illegitimate; and if the mother was a widow, he is "kosher." In the absence of other sources concerning the husband's fate, the burning question is whether her own testimony is admissible. The fact that she was a single witness and a woman – whereas Jewish law usually demands two male witness – was accepted here, while the validity of her knowledge at times of war and personal turmoil was the rabbi's concern. The Egyptian Jews that submitted the query had no doubt that she was from "the seed of Israel."

Another major facet of this episode is the master's attitude towards the slave. Contemporaneous slave owners evidently took liberties with their female chattel. In fact, there are documents referring to the offspring of these sort of relationships who eventually became members in good standing of the Jewish community. Moreover, "black" and "Nubian" are known synonyms for the word "slave" in Medieval Arabic and Judeo-Arabic. At least in all that concerned the master in the case at hand, the Kushite's skin color apparently took precedence over her Jewishness.[7] What is more, her double status, as a black Jewess, was a detriment to the child, for there is no easy remedy for the label of *mamzer*. On the other hand, if the boy had been classified as the progeny of a non-Jewish slave, he could have readily undergone a conversion.

Ben Zimra divides his answer into two. First, after deliberating over this matter, he concludes that the woman's testimony as to her husband's fate is immaterial. Consequently, she is deemed to be a married woman – an *agunah* – and the child she had with Reuben is a bastard. The rest of ben Zimra's answer pertains to the woman's Jewishness. From the text, it is clear that the leader aspired to conduct a principled discussion on "this nation," that is Ethiopian Jewry. In my estimation, there are two major strands to his argument. To begin with, ben Zimra considers the Beta-Israel as Karaites – a point stressed by many of his counterparts and researchers. Ben Zimra reached this conclusion on the basis of his determination that they "do not know the oral law and do not light candles on Sabbath eve." Other references to the Beta-Israel in the adjudicator's works indicate that he arrived at this information through his own or a colleague's personal contact and familiarity with this group. Secondly, ben Zimra is certain that they "are Israelites from the tribe of Dan" who were banished either immediately before or after the first Temple's destruction. By equating the Beta-Israel with "the sect of Zadok and Boethus who are referred to as Karaites," he even appears to be reconciling between these two designations. More specifically, ben Zimra contends that Ethiopian Jews are tied to sects from the second Temple period that both Karaites and Rabbinites identified as the progenitors of the former. Be that as it may, the Danites and Karaites are not identical. From ben Zimra's standpoint, this point is critical, for it opens the door to the Beta-Israel's reintegration into Rabbinite Judaism. He then demonstrates at considerable length that the eons that have passed since the group's exile negate the possibility that its marriage ceremonies adhered to Jewish law. In consequence, the Beta-Israel are not *mamzers*.

This logic might seem odd to the modern reader: the "less Jewish" that the Beta-Israel are (i.e., they were not married according to the Rabbinic tradition), the "easier" it is from a legalistic-Rabbinic perspective to accept them into the fold of mainstream Judaism and wed its members. During the time of this incident, Karaites were "rebelling" against the Rabbinite leadership's authority. Since the same cannot be said for Ethiopian Jewry, ben Zimra opined that "if all of them were to agree to enter the religion of the fellowship [i.e., the Rabbinite stream], to take upon themselves the traditions of our rabbis of blessed memory, [and] to be like us, I would allow them to enter the community with the sages' approval." Put differently, were the Beta-Israel to embrace the oral law and were the rest of the generation's luminaries to accept them, ben Zimra would welcome them back into mainstream Jewish society. As an aside, it is worth noting that this is ultimately what happened over the course of the twentieth century, albeit in an unwitting and inadvertent manner.

In another responsum concerning "a freed slave from those same Jews residing in the Land of Kush," ben Zimra revisits the subject of this community's Jewishness. Toughening his earlier stance, the adjudicator underscores the difference between the Karaites who "see [*sic*] the teachings of the sages and denigrate and scorn them" and "those who come from the Land of Kush [who] are undoubtedly from the tribe of Dan." "Inasmuch as none of their sages," the adjudicator reasons, "possessed the [oral] tradition, a literal [interpretation] of the writ took hold of them. But had they been taught [the oral law] they would not have denied the words of our rabbis of blessed memory." Furthermore, ben Zimra notes that "Zadok and Boethus were indeed in the second Temple and the tribe of Dan was exiled before [its destruction]."[8] In any event, he is now concerned that perhaps the Beta-Israel's marriage ceremonies, as opposed to their divorces, did adhere to Jewish law. If so, the problem of *mamzer*s is back on the table. Halakhically speaking, then, having part in a post-temple, "Talmudic," Judaism again places obstacles before the community.

With respect to the topic at hand, it is noteworthy that ben Zimra accepts and makes sense of Ethiopian Jewry by compartmentalizing them under two headings that were germane during his lifetime: the Karaites and the tribe of Dan. The Karaites posed a religious and social problem for the Egyptian Rabbinite community; and as we have seen, European Jews that settled in the Near East during the century before ben Zimra's own arrival were captivated by the search for the Israelites and Prester John. Furthermore, my impression from the relevant texts is that ben Zimra was influenced by Eldad's account of the Ten Tribes. According to the Egyptian Rabbi, "there is a constant war between the kings of Kush, which consists of three monarchies – some of it Ishmaelite and some of it Arameans that are true to their faith, and some of it are Israelites from the tribe of Dan ... And the war between them will not cease, and prisoners are taken from both sides every day." It stands to reason that these hostilities between Muslims, Christians, and Jews echo the historic events in Ethiopia during ben Zimra's age. In my estimation, though, this static-cum-eternal conflict hints to the Eldad's stories about the Lost Tribes (see chapter 2). Likewise, the word "nation" (*umah*), which ben Zimra uses to describe the Beta-Israel, is commonplace in Eldad's writings.[9]

From hereon in, the topic of Ethiopian Jewry's affiliation with the Danites became a fixture of the rabbinical-Halakhic discourse. While augmenting his knowledge from the works of non-Jewish geographers, even a critical Jewish thinker like Azariah de Rossi (1511–1578) depended on Eldad and his stories in portraying the Jews of Ethiopia. In de Rossi's estimation, though, the exiled Israelites headed off in the direction of Assyria, not the Horn of Africa. More specifically, he opined that the Beta-Israel splintered off from the Ten Tribes and whole-heartedly equates them with the sons of Moses residing beyond the Sambation River – a clear allusion to Eldad's tales.[10] Surprising as it may be, this identification was bolstered in the 1800s by the scholars of the *Wissenschaft des Judentums* – the German-Jewish movement that raised the banner of academically and critically examining Judaism and its history.

It was semi-ethnographic adventurers-cum-explorers that revealed Ethiopia to Occidental audiences. First and foremost among these travelers was James Bruce (1730–1794), who set out to find the source of the Nile and returned with, among other things, compelling information on Ethiopian culture. He also reported on an encounter with the "Falasha" – the descendants of King Solomon and Queen Sheba. That said, direct contact between European and Ethiopian Jewry was initially established by the French geographer Antoine Thomson d'Abbadie (1810–1897), who spent seven years in the African kingdom. In 1845, d'Abbadie reported on his findings in the French press, including an account of a meeting with a Beta-Israel clergyman Abba Issak (Father Isaac) and members of his congregation. Among those who read this dispatch was one Filosseno Luzzatto (1829–1854) – the teenaged son of the Italian-Jewish intellectual Samuel David Luzzatto (1800–1865). With the help of Italian messengers, Filosseno sent d'Abbadie a batch of questions for Abba Issak. Twenty-eight months later, the answers were published in a Parisian Jewish press. Filosseno subsequently collected all the available information on the "Jews of Abyssinia" from letters by geographers – foremost among them d'Abbadie – and other scholars for the sake of writing a book on this topic.[11]

Owing to his untimely death the young researcher did not complete this project. For instance, Luzzatto never managed to formulate his position on the origins of the Beta-Israel. However, a careful reading of the posthumously published book suggests that he was inclined to believe that the Beta-Israel arrived in Ethiopia from either the Land of Israel or Egypt during the first century CE. For this reason, Filosseno averred that their dating of the first Temple's destruction is more credible than mainstream Jewish estimates and accords with the chronology in the Bible. Moreover, he concluded that Ethiopian Jews practiced a Biblical religion whose main pillars were observance of the Sabbath, kashrut, laws of purification and defilement, *niddah*, scriptural festivals and fast days, sacrifices, and extreme segregation from non-Jews. Yet another Biblical dimension of their lore was the belief that the community's founders were part of the retinue that had accompanied Queen Sheba on her return from Judea (or King Menelik, after being sent to study in Jerusalem with his father King Salomon). Filosseno Luzzatto's enterprise was indeed nipped in the bud, but his father would assume the torch in fulfillment of his child's last wishes.

Despite the voices of objectors,[12] the Beta-Israel henceforth became a significant political and social issue in the Jewish discourse. Furthermore, the interest in and contacts with the Beta-Israel steadily gained momentum.

Let us restrict ourselves to the intellectual sphere. To a certain degree, it was Abraham Epstein who disclosed an unspoken assumption concerning Eldad the Danite and Ethiopian Jewry and who forged a lasting bond between the two. A distinguished and prolific scholar,

Epstein assembled, organized, sorted, and expounded on all the versions of Eldad's writings in a single tract. This work still constitutes the lynchpin for every discussion on Eldad (see chapter 2). Additionally, Epstein fashioned an independent study on "the Falashas and their Culture"[13] according to which the Danite and Beta-Israel clearly illuminate one another. Already in the preface to this book, the scholar echoed ben Zimra's argument that remote Jewish communities "would not have intentionally objected to the oral law like the Sadducees and Karaites; only on account of this lack of knowledge did they innocently conduct themselves according to the biblical views that were accepted in their community from the time of their departure from … their brethren in order to wander far and wide." Moreover, he opined on the connection between the Danite and the Jews of Ethiopia:

> I have seen that Eldad's writings tell of Jews unbeknownst to us …
> It seems from [the] content [of the Danite's work] that they [i.e., the
> Lost Tribes] are not a figment of his imagination and [the customs
> he described] were practiced somewhere by Jews who did not know
> much from the Talmud. In his stories about the life of the Tribes,
> there are a couple of things that are still practiced today by the Jews
> in Abyssinia, as I demonstrated in the introduction … [Therefore,] I
> took the trouble to affix a paper on the Falasha, who have been
> living closed off and trapped in Abyssinia for thousands of years. In
> addition, observing their customs brings appreciable benefit to
> understanding the evolution of the oral law, especially after I found
> therein a couple of practices that are mentioned by Eldad.[14]

While jettisoning the identification that had taken root since ben Zimra's ruling, Epstein seems to have offered a plausible research approach. In his estimation, the link between the Danite and the Beta-Israel is merely a coincidental historico-contextual resemblance that was bolstered by geographical proximity. The scholar's far-reaching innovation places the spotlight on the oral law. Eldad clearly had a post-Biblical tradition – one that Epstein also detected in the hands of the Beta-Israel. For this reason, the correlation that he drew between Eldad and the Beta-Israel, partial as it may be, speaks volumes on the question of their Jewishness and reabsorption into the bosom of Rabbinic Judaism. Epstein concluded that Eldad was from an actual community in South Yemen, or one that was tied to (or broke off from) Yemenite Jewry, but resided on the other side of the Gulf of Aden (present-day Somalia).[15] His discussion on Beta-Israel opens with the suggestion that their ancestors also crossed the gulf and settled on the

African coast, before sojourning inland and traversing the mountains into Ethiopia.[16] At the end of the work, though, he concluded that only a small portion of the Beta-Israel had arrived from Yemen. Instead, the majority were "members of the Ten Tribes, the Samaritans, and ... [the tribes of] Judah and Benjamin" who came from Egypt, where they dwelled in the centuries immediately before and after the Common Era.[17]

The tacit premise of his discussion on Ethiopian Jewry is that the community possessed some sort of oral law (or "Targim," a term he found in James Bruce's report). Epstein repeatedly contrasted and compared elements of this tradition to Jewish post-Temple traditions.[18] Furthermore, he sought to project from their lore onto the essence of the Rabbinic learnings. A case in point is his disquisition on the source of the commandment to don phylacteries (*tefillin*) and its connection to the Beta-Israel practice of etching various talismans on the human body. The impetus behind this discussion was a remark about phylacteries that d'Abbadie heard from a Beta-Israel clergyman. According to the latter, this ritual is not practiced in Ethiopia because the local tattooing dye is not very strong and the inscription of the Ten Commandments on their arms would soon wear off. Epstien deducts from this that practice to tattoo magical names is the origin of the commandment on phylacteries, and this is how they were first practiced.[19]

Despite his caution, virtue of his deep familiarity with Eldad's writings, Epstein avertedly solidified Eldad's link to the Beta-Israel, especially tying his "oral law" – "the Talmud of the Tribes" – to the community's traditions, rituals, and praxis. As a result of Epstein's insights, many scholars, lucking Epstein's erudition and caution, were persuaded that there is an affinity between Eldad and the Ethiopian Jews. A case in point is the entry "Falasha" in the *Jewish Encyclopedia* from 1906, blending everything together:

> In Hebrew writings there are only a few and, in general, indistinct references to the Falashas. The earliest account is in the diary of Eldad the Danite (9th cent.). His account, especially of the halakhot of the Abyssinian Jews, has been carefully studied by A. Epstein ('Eldad ha-Dani,' Pressburg 1891).[20]

This view was destined to fill a major role in the State of Israel's decision concerning the Jewishness of the Beta-Israel.

As a condition for recognizing the Beta-Israel as Jews, the first chief rabbis of the state of Israel, Isaac Herzog and Ben-Zion Meir Hai Uziel, demanded that they undergo a conversion – a position that even

Faitlovitch supported – and attend rabbinically-supervised education (primarily Uziel). Herzog ruled that the Jews of Ethiopia are the off-spring of proselytes, but their conversion process failed to meet Orthodox standards. For this reason, the Ashkenazi chief rabbi was concerned that "Perhaps they are not Jews in the Halakhic sense" of the word. As noted above, this position could ultimately facilitate the Beta-Israel's acceptance into Israeli society, so long as they acquiesced to an Orthodox conversion. In fact, the first emigrants to enroll in Jewish schools, under Faitlovitch's mediation, underwent a lenient conversion process. Given the fact that they were already circumcised, the authorities sufficed with the drawing of a symbolic drop of "cove-nantal blood."[21] The Israeli Rabbinate indeed demanded that the son of Jeremiah Getya – the Beta-Israel teen that Faitlovitch brought to Florence after his maiden trip to Ethiopia in 1904 and who then returned home to teach Judaism – go through this process before deigning to administer a marriage ceremony on his behalf. In 1966, the Israeli Supreme Court ruled that the Rabbinate was within its bounds to convert Getya's son on the grounds that the Beta-Israels are not Jewish. Among other sources, the judges predicated their decision on rabbinical and scholarly opinions (e.g., that of Edward Ullendorff, a fellow of the British Academy who edited the Hebrew version of Pre-ster John's letters).[22]

The Rabbinate's position on the Jewishness of the Beta-Israel took a surprising turn in a ruling that was issued by Ovadia Yosef, the Sephardic chief rabbi, in 1973. Responding to questions that were submitted to him, Yosef promulgated that "the Falashas are Jews" on the basis of precedents set by ben Zimra, R. Yaakov de Castro (ben Zimra's disciple and successor), R. Raphael Meir Panigel (the Ottoman head of the Palestine Jewish community in the late 1800s), and R. Azriel Hildesheimer (among the founders of Modern Orthodox Judaism). More specifically, the adjudicator concluded that Ethiopian Jews "are from the tribe of Dan ... according to the most credible testimonies and evidence."[23] Although Shlomo Goren, the coeval Ashkenazic chief rabbi, disagreed with this ruling, the state applied the Law of Return to Ethiopian Jewry, thereby enabling them to emigrate and become citizens of Israel. Moreover, Yosef's opinion paved the way for the full absorp-tion of the Beta-Israel into Israeli society.

Be that as it may, the Israeli Rabbinate insisted that the Beta-Israel undergo conversion ceremonies, which were dubbed *ḥidush ha-brit* ("renewal of the covenant"). Though lenient, these rituals were unpre-cedented even from a Rabbinite Halakhic standpoint. In essence, it was a reincarnation of the ceremony described in the Book of Nehemiah (chapters 8–10). Within this framework, three demands were made of the African candidates: to undergo "covenantal blood-letting;" take upon themselves the commandments of the Torah; and subject themselves to ritual immersion. Following the waves of emigration from Ethiopia in the 1980s, young members of the community rebelled against these stipulations. The Rabbinate came their way and abrogated the blood-letting component, but the very insistence on a ceremony roils members of the Beta-Israel to this day and age.

While Yosef's ruling dovetailed neatly with the Jewish nationalism in Israel at the time and was accepted by the Israeli public, it posed major difficulties from a Halakhic perspective. If the Beta-Israel are indeed Jews, there was a concern that the group's weddings, as opposed to its divorces, were performed in accordance to Orthodox law. This, then, raised the possibility that the Beta-Israel are *mamzers* and thus forbidden from marrying Jews.[24] With this in mind, a number of senior rabbis, such as R. Moshe Feinstein (the twentieth century's leading Halakhic authority in the United States) and R. Eliezer Waldenberg (a jurist on the Supreme Rabbinical Court of Israel) ruled against Yosef and demanded that the Ethiopian emigrants undergo a thorough conversion process.[25]

In 1985, this dispute compelled Ovadia Yosef to publish a clarification on the matter of the Beta-Israel's Jewishness.[26] To begin with, the rabbi noted that his original letter from 1973 – the text of which was added as a footnote to the updated ruling – paved the way for the state's decision to apply the Law of Return to the Beta-Israel. Furthermore, he solved the problem of marrying Ethiopian Jews and contended with a litany of critiques against his initial decision. Yosef's opinion is premised on the unmitigated acceptance of ben Zimra's testimony, along with a sweeping rejection of every study that questions Ethiopian Jewry's Danite origins. In the first place, he took issue with Herzog's above-mentioned argument whereby the Beta-Israel are the scion of converts:

> Terrible is my astonishment over what he [i.e., Herzog] saw to reject in this fashion the opinions of world class geniuses that have established with certitude that there is no doubt that they are from the tribe of Dan because of the words of researchers casting doubt on their Jewishness; and who, I wonder, overrides who [in this debate]!?[27]

Similarly, Yosef rebuffed Waldenberg's opinion on the grounds that his main source – the orthodox encyclopedia *Ozar Yisrael* (Julius Eisenstein, New York 1907–1913) – leans on the testimony of Christian

travelers. Contrasting Waldenberg's ruling with his own, Yosef emphasized the fact that he had spoken with members of the Beta-Israel
themselves, who told him that they had intentionally concealed truths
about their faith from non-Jewish neighbors.

> Is it possible, that one can rely on a study of this sort [i.e., one based
> on non-Rabbinic sources] to cast doubt on the Jewishness of an entire
> community that put their lives on the line for the belief in a single
> God and his Torah as per the tradition of their forefathers and to
> damage the presumption of their Jewishness that has been established
> in accordance with the testimony of the geniuses of yesteryear.

On more than one occasion, the former chief rabbi stated that ben
Zimra and de Castro are trustworthy witnesses beyond reproof, whose
Halakhic prowess far outshines that of their successors. Leaning on
what he sees as a universal consensus surrounding ben Zimra's great-
ness, Yosef repudiates the objection of R. Moshe Feinstein, who
implied that perhaps the sixteenth-century rabbi was not fully apprised
of the Beta-Israel's situation.

Ovadia Yosef's reliance on the opinion of ben Zimra and de Castro
may very well have been tinged with personal affinity. As the former
deputy-chief rabbi of Egypt between 1947 and 1950, Yosef certainly felt a
bond with these two erstwhile heads of the Egyptian Jewish community.
Likewise, it is possible that Yosef's adamant opposition to "the research"
betrays his ideological and temperamental differences *vis-à-vis* Chaim
Nahum Effendi, the chief rabbi of Egypt from 1925 to 1960. The latter
authored an inordinately negative scientific study about the Beta-Israel
for *Alliance israélite universelle*, the French Jewish organization, in
1908.[28] Given the absence of firm evidence, this psychological conjecture
must be taken with a grain of salt. At any rate, Yosef manifests that the
legend of Eldad the Danite and the identification between the latter and
Beta-Israel had already become Rabbinic dogma.

Having unreservedly established that the Beta-Israel are of Danite
descent, Ovadia Yosef grappled with the problem of marrying the
community's members – a topic to which he devoted the lion's share of
his responsum. On the basis of conversations with and queries from
Ethiopian Jews, he ascertained that their weddings indeed diverge from
"the faith of Moses and Israel," namely Talmudic Halakha. This discovery indeed negates the possibility that the Beta-Israel are *mamzers*.
As a result, there is no need for Beta-Israel divorcees to secure a *get*
(writ of divorce); and even if a couple separated and remarried, their
children from that point forward are not defined as bastards. In reaching

this conclusion, Yosef distinguished between the Beta-Israel and groups that distanced themselves from the Rabbinite stream over the course of Jewish history, such as the "Kutim" (i.e., Samaritans), the Karaites, and the Converso. Insofar as he was concerned, the Ethiopian Jews' Israelite origins and attendant remoteness from the Talmudic tradition worked in their favor on the question of nuptials and also facilitated their absorption into the Jewish state. The Rabbi end with a univocal ruling:

> "We have searched high and low, so that there is no need to ponder the obviation of officiating weddings in the Ethiopian community, and they are permitted to enter Jewish society in good standing without converting even *le-ḥumra* [a stringent approach to Torah observance that goes beyond the letter of the law]."

Yosef, who had no compunctions against locking horns with savants past and present, accepted the identification of Ethiopian Jewry with the tribe of Dan as an incontrovertible Halakhic truth. As opposed to his predecessors, he leveraged Beta-Israel's foreignness and aberrancy – the fact that they lack the oral law – to completely integrate them into the Jewish fold. This is perhaps why Yosef made no mention whatsoever of Eldad or his "Talmud" in his decision. The rabbi's approach stands in contradistinction to peers who predicated their acceptance of the Beta-Israel's Jewishness to the testimony offered by Eldad, as the authentic representative of the Danites and one that also came from Ethiopia – "the Land of Kush."[29] Nevertheless, in order to establish Yosef's estimation, there is no practical Halakhic difference as to which of the Ten Tribes the Beta-Israel derive from, be it Zebulun, Issachar, Gad, or Reuben. Consequently, his decision to associate the Beta-Israel with the Danites, which he inherited from ben Zimra, is a less than subtle allusion to the Eldadian corpus. The reason he neglects to mention this connection out loud is the same for those who emphasized it: Eldad's oral traditions, his so-called Talmud – once a proof of Beta-Israel's Jewishness, and now an obstacle in their acceptance.

From the sixteenth to the twentieth century, the Beta-Israel gradually came to be identified with Eldad the Danite. While ben Zimra and Ovadia Yosef spearheaded the Beta-Israel's acceptance into Orthodox Judaism, it was the affiliation with the lost tribe of Dan, established by the myth of Eldad, that hide behind their efforts. Following their arrival to Israel, the Beta-Israel even adopted the tribe of Dan as their forbearer and preferred this narrative to their community's age-old tradition as the descendants of King Solomon and Queen Sheba. In turn, they projected their own image onto Eldad, to the point where today many believe that this legendary ninth-century figure was a black Jew from Ethiopia.

Notes

1 In the Hebrew original, we encounter the acronym *bet-hei*. Our assumption is that it stands for *beit ha-knesset* (synagogue).

2 E.g., Tudor Parfitt, "Construction of Jewish Identities in Africa," in Parfitt and Emanuela Trevisan Semi, eds., *Jews of Ethiopia: The Birth of an Elite* (London and New York 2005), 34 (cf. 188–189).

3 Steven Kaplan, *The Beta Israel (Falasha) in Ethiopia: From Earliest Times to the Twentieth Century* (New York and London 1992), 53–78, 155–166.

4 Faitlovitch studied in France under the Orientalist Joseph Halévy, who had also endeavored, albeit with less success, to forge ties with Ethiopia Jewry.

5 See Moti Benmelech, "Beyond the Sambatyon: Changes in the Image of the Ten Tribes and Expectations for their Return in the Early Modern Times," *Zion* 77 (2012): 491–527 [Hebrew].

6 *Responsa of the RaDBaZ*, part IV (Jerusalem 1972), § 219 (1,000–290), 119–120 [Hebrew].

7 This is perhaps what Yaakov de Castro, the RaDBaZ's disciple, was hinting to in what is likely another responsum on this same episode: "And there already was … a case of a Habesha Jewess who was married in her land; and she gave birth in Egypt to a son from a Jewish man who **inadvertently** (*bi-shegaga*) had intercourse with her. Thereafter, the son married a female servant and purified his seed, in the time of the sages of the generation before us." De Castro, *The Responsa of Jacob's Tents*, §11 [Hebrew].

8 *Responsa of the RaDBaZ*, ibid., part VII ('ruling considering *agunot*'), §5, pp. 6–7.

9 Menachem Valdman offers a detailed portrait, as well as a conclusion that differs from my own; idem, *Beyond the Rivers of Ethiopia* (Tel Aviv 1989), 74–76 [Hebrew]. Also see Aaron Zeev Aescoly, *The Book of the Falashas* (Jerusalem 1972), 166–167 [Hebrew].

10 Azariah dei Rossi, *Me'or Einayim*, part III, Imrei binah, chapter 13 [Hebrew].

11 Philoxéne Luzzatto, *Mémoire sur les Juifs d'Abyssinie ou Falashas*, Extrait des Archives Israélites (Paris 1852).

12 E.g., Haïm Nahoum, "Mission chez les Falachas d'Abyssinie," *Bulletin de l'Alliance israélite universelle* 33/3 (1908): 100–137.

13 The German title page reads thus: *Eldad ha-Dani: seine Berichte über die X Stämme und deren Ritus…nebst einem Excurse über die Falascha und deren Bebräuche* (Pressburg 1891). A. M. Haberman published a moderately revised version of this book in Epstein's collected works: *Works of R. Abraham Epstein*.

14 Ibid., v–vi.

15 Ibid., xix.

16 Ibid., 141–142.

17 Ibid., 187–189.

18 Ibid., 144, 148–149, 167–170, 173–174, *inter alia*.

19 Ibid., 174–183.

20 Richard Gottheil and Jean Michel Perruchon, "Falasha," *Jewish Encyclopedia* (1906). Also see Parfitt and Trevisan Semi, eds., *Jews of Ethiopia: The Birth of an Elite*. Another example is the Italian scholar of Ethiopian culture: Carlo Conti Rossini, *Leggende geografiche guidaich del IX secolo (Il Sefer Eldad)*, *Bollettino della reale Società Georafice Italiana* VI (Roma, 1925).

21 Valdman, *Beyond the Rivers of Ethiopia*, 250–253.
22 Ibid., 272–274.
23 Israel State Archive, file A-11/114 [Hebrew]; Valdman, ibid., 276. As noted, the letter was also inserted into the footnotes of the responsa *Yabia omer*; see below.
24 See Valdman, "Marriage and Divorce among Ethiopian Jewry," *Teḥumin* 11 (1990): 214–240 [Hebrew]; Shlomo Amar, "On the Matter of Ethiopian Jewry's Kashrut," *Beit Hilllel* year 4, vol. 3 (16) (2003): 36–44 [Hebrew].
25 It is worth noting that unlike Waldenberg, Feinstein designed his ruling with the intention of facilitating Ethiopian Jewry's absorption into Israeli society.
26 Ovadia Yosef, *Yabia omer*, part VIII, 'Righteous among the Nations,' §11.
27 Elsewhere in this responsum, Yosef unleashed another volley at the scholarship: "I am shocked … that he [i.e., Waldenberg] endeavors to reject the testimony of world-class geniuses on account [of] researchers whose words are less than vapor … After that rabbi Ben Zimra and R. de Castro expressly ruled that they are from the tribe of Dan, who is and where is the person with the wherewithal to set out against an entire community [in an effort] to invalidate them and leave a blemish on [their] marriage ceremonies."
28 Nahoum, "Mission chez les Falachas d'Abyssinie."
29 For example, David Slush, *May the Outcast of Israel Assemble: On Ethiopian Jewry* (Jerusalem 1988), 11–19, 110–111 [Hebrew].

Conclusion

This book has traced the transmission of the image of Eldad and the texts attributed to this figure – from his initial appearance in ninth-century Kairouan to the modern state of Israel. In the process, we have attempted to present various applications of the historian's craft. While philology allowed us to establish the very existence of Eldad, literary criticism helped us to uncover the ideological message that Eldad brought to the Jewish diaspora at a crucial point in its development. Following the transmission and transformation of the texts ascribed to Eldad has unveiled how its audience understood, read, and used them across time, thus exposing contemporaneous ideology and theology, as well as practical concerns and values. The resulting portrait shows Rabbanites, Karaites, Christians, men and women('s advocates), each reading Eldad through the prism of their own aspirations. Finally, our examination of the identification of Beta-Israel with Eldad has enabled us to map out a transnational history of sorts, as we traversed geographic borders and cultural boundaries across time and space, as well as the social divide between rabbis and scholars.

On the one hand, the case of Eldad the Danite is unique; on the other, however, it is representative of a much larger picture. His literature is unique because of its mythical connection to the Ten Lost Tribes and to famed medieval marvels, as well as his claim to have brought traditions directly from the mouth of Moses on Mt. Sinai. Nevertheless, through these very singularities, Eldad allows us to peek at transformations in Jewish culture, offering a glimpse of historical processes that usually are hidden from the eye. These developments encapsulate the story of Jewish culture from the Middle Ages through modernity: first, the victory of the Babylonian tradition over its counterparts; then, the centuries-long unification of Jewish traditions into one governing body of knowledge; and, finally, despite this tendency, the absorption of new traditions, at times extremely distant, such as Beta-Israel, into a single overarching culture.

The course of Jewish history, as portrayed through the transmission of the Eldadian corpus, narrates how disparate traditions can co-exist in what might be termed "cultural globalization." The success of such instance relies on the ability to incorporate ever-changing local traditions within larger, even global, stable boundaries, thus fostering unification through diversity. This dynamic epitomizes the story of Jewish culture up to modern times: the ability to rewrite, interpret, and adapt to changing times, while maintaining shared boundaries.

The transformations of Eldad and his myth have not yet reached their end: Ethiopian Jewish youth in Israel increasingly ascribe him significance (alongside Haile Selassie and Bob Marley); the Igbo tribe of Nigeria base their claim to Jewish identity in part on the tales of Eldad; it is rumored that the personage of Amram, the Abyssinian giant in Michael Chabon's *Gentlemen of the Road*, is inspired by the image of Eldad; and, hopefully, this book too, all attest to the enduring charms of Eldad and his story.

Bibliography

Aescoly, Aaron Zeev. *Jewish Messianic Movements*. Jerusalem: 1987 [Hebrew].

Aescoly, Aaron Zeev. *The Book of the Falashas*. Jerusalem: 1972 [Hebrew].

Amar, Shlomo. "On the Matter of Ethiopian Jewry's Kashru." *Beit Hilllel* year 4, vol. 3 (16) (2003): 36–44 [Hebrew].

Anderson, Andrew R. *Alexander's Gate, Gog and Magog, and the Inclosed Nations*. Monographs of the Medieval Academy of America, no. 5. Cambridge, MA: 1932.

Bale, Anthony. *The Book of Marvels and Travels*. Oxford: 2012.

Baraz, Daniel. *Medieval Cruelty: Changing Perceptions, Late Antiquity to the Early Modern Period*. Ithaca: 2003.

Baron, Salo W. *A Social and Religious History of the Jews*. Second edition, revised and enlarged. New York: 1958.

Baron, Salo W. *The Jewish Community: Its History and Structure to the American Revolution*, vol. II. Philadelphia: 1942.

Baumgarten, Elisheva. "'And They do Nicely:' A Reappraisal of Menstruation. Women's Refusal to Enter the Sanctuary in Medieval Ashkenaz." In Avraham Reiner et al., *Ta Shma: Studies in Memory of Israel M. Ta-Shma*. Alon Shevut, Israel: 2011, 85–104 [Hebrew].

Baumgarten, Elisheva. *Mothers and Children: Jewish Family Life in Medieval Europe*. Princeton: 2004.

Beckingham, Charles F. "The Achievements of Prester John." In Charles F. Beckingham and Bernard Hamilton, eds. *Prester John, the Mongols and the Ten Lost Tribes*, 1–24.

Beckingham, Charles F. and Bernard Hamilton, eds. *Prester John, the Mongols and the Ten Lost Tribes*. Aldershot, Hampshire: 1996.

Bejczy, István. *La lettre du Prêtre Jean: une utopie médiévale*. Paris: 2001.

Ben-Dor Benite, Zvi. *The Ten Lost Tribes: A World History*. Oxford: 2009.

Benmelech, Moti. "Beyond the Sambatyon: Changes in the Image of the Ten Tribes and Expectations for their Return in the Early Modern Times." *Zion* 77 (2012): 491–527 [Hebrew].

Benmelech, Moti. *Shlomo Molcho: The Life and Death of Messiah Ben Joseph.* Jerusalem: 2016 [Hebrew].

Ben-Sasson, Menahem. *Emergence of the Local Jewish Community in the Muslim World, Qayrawan, 800-1057.* Jerusalem: 1996 [Hebrew].

Bonfil, Robert. "Between Eretz Israel and Babylonia." *Shalem* 5 (1987): 1–30 [Hebrew].

Bonfil, Robert. "The Cultural and Religious Traditions of French Jewry in the Ninth Century, as Reflected in the Writings of Agobard of Lyons." *Studies in Jewish Mysticism, Philosophy and Ethical Literature, Presented to Isaiah Tishby.* Jerusalem: 1986, 327–348 [Hebrew].

Bonfil, Robert. "The Devil and the Jews in the Christian Consciousness of the Middle Ages." In Shmuel Almog, ed., *Antisemitism through the Ages.* Oxford: 1988, 91–98.

Bonfil, Robert. "The Historian's Perception of the Jews in the Italian Renaissance: Toward a Reappraisal." *REJ* 143 (1984): 59–82.

Boureau, Alain. *The Lord's First Night.* Translated by Lydia G. Cochrane. Chicago: 1998.

Boureau, Alain. *The Myth of Pope Joan.* Translated by Lydia G. Cochrane. Chicago: 2001.

Brewer, Keagan. *Prester John: The Legend and its Sources. Crusade Texts in Translation,* vol. 27. Farnham: 2015.

Brody, Robert. *Readings in Geonic Literature.* Tel Aviv: 1998 [Hebrew].

Brody, Robert. *The Geonim of Babylonia and the Shaping of Medieval Jewish Culture.* Yale: 1998.

Carta do Preste João das Índias: Versões medievais Latinas. Translated by L. Buescu. Lisbon: 1998.

Cohen, Jeremy. "Antichrist and His Jewish Connections." In *Rishonim ve-Achronim: Studies in Jewish History Presented to Avraham Grossman.* Jerusalem: 2010, 29–45.

Cohen, Jeremy. *Living Letters of the Law: Ideas of the Jew in Medieval Christianity.* Berkeley: 1999.

Cohen, Jeremy. *Sanctifying the Name of God: Jewish Memories of the First Crusade.* Philadelphia: 2004.

Colorni, V. "Abraham Conat, primo stampatore di opere ebraiche in Mantova e la cronologia delle sue edizioni." *La Bibliofilía* 83/2 (1981): 113–128.

Conti, Rossini Carlo. *Leggende geografiche guidaich del IX secolo (Il Sefer Eldad). Bollettino della reale Società Georafice Italiana.* VI, Roma: 1925.

Danzig, Neil. *Introduction to Halakhot Pesuqot.* New York: 1993 [Hebrew].

Dinari, Yedidya Alter. *The Rabbis of Germany and Austria at the Close of the Middle Ages.* Jerusalem: 1984 [Hebrew].

Duschinsky, Charles. "May a Woman Act as Shoheteth?" In Bruno Schindler, ed., *Occident and Orient. Gaster Anniversary Volume.* London: 1936, 96–106.

Eisenstein, Judah D. *Ozar Wikuhim: A Collection of Polemics and Disputations.* New York: 1928.

Elazar ben Judah of Worms. *The Commentary on the Prayer Book of the Rokheach.* Edited by Moshe Hershler and Yehudah Alter Hershler. Jerusalem: 1992 [Hebrew].

Elkin, Zeev. "The Karaite Version of Sefer ha-Ḥilluqim bein Benei Erez-Yisrael le-Benei Bavel." *Tarbiẓ* 66/1 (October-December1996): 101–111 [Hebrew].

Emanuel, Simcha. *Fragments of the Tablets: Lost Books of the Toasaphists.* Jerusalem: 2006 [Hebrew].

Emanuel, Simcha. "Rabbi Baruch of Mainz – Portrait of a Scholar as Reflected in the Fragments of His Writings." In *Issues in Talmudic Research, Conference Commemorating the Fifth Anniversary of the Passing of Ephraim E. Urbach, 2 December 1996.* Jerusalem: 2001, 124–163 [Hebrew].

Epstein, Abraham. *Kitvei R. Avraham Epstein.* Edited by Abraham Meir Habermann, 2 vols. Jerusalem: 1950 [Hebrew].

Epstein, Abraham. *Sefer Eldad ha-Dani.* Vienna: 1891.

Epstein, Jacob N. "The Lore of Erez Israel: Traifot." *Tarbiẓ* 2/3 (April 1931): 308–327 [Hebrew].

Fishman, Talya. *Becoming People of the Talmud.* Philadelphia: 2011.

Funkenstein, Amos. *Perceptions of Jewish History.* Berkeley: 1993.

Gluska, Yitzchak. "Eldad the Danite of Yemen and the Language of His Writing." In Aharaon Gaimani et al., eds., *Sons of Yemen: Studies on Yemenite Jewry and its Heritage*, Ramat Gan: 2011, 137–268 [Hebrew].

Gosman, Martin. *La lettre du Prêtre Jean: les versions en ancien français et en ancien occitan, textes et commentaires.* Groningen: 1982.

Gow, Andrew C. *The Red Jews: Antisemitism in an Apocalyptic Age 1200–1600. Studies in Medieval and Reformation Thought*, vol. LV. Leiden: 1995.

Graetz, Heinrich. *History of the Jews from the Earliest Times to the Present Day.* The Saul Pinchas Rabbinowicz edition. Warsaw: 1896.

Grayzel, Solomon. *The Church and the Jews in the XIIIth Century*, vol. 2: "1254–1314," Edited by Kenneth R. Stow. New York: 1989.

Grossman, Avraham. *Pious and Rebellious: Jewish Women in Medieval Europe.* Translated by Jonathan Chipman. Waltham, MA: 2005.

Grossman, Avraham. *The Early Sages of Ashkenaz.* Jerusalem: 1981 [Hebrew].

Gross, Abraham. "The Expulsion and the Search for the Ten Tribes." *Judaism* 41/2 (1992): 130–147.

Gross, Abraham. "The Ten Tribes and the Kingdom of Prester John – Rumors and Investigations before and after the Expulsion from Spain." *Pe'amim* 48 (1991): 5–41 [Hebrew].

Hadassi, Judah. *Eshkol ha-kofer.* Gözleve [Yevpatoria]: 1836.

Halakhot Psukot. S. Sassoon edition, Makize Nirdamim. Jerusalem: 1951 [Hebrew].

Hamilton, Bernard. "Prester John and the Three Kings of Cologne." In Henry Mayr-Harting and Robert Ian Moore, eds., *Studies in Medieval History Presented to R. H. C. Davis.* London: 1985, 171–185.

Haverkamp, Eva (Hg.). *Hebräische Berichte über die Judenverfolgungen während des Ersten Kreuzzugs.* Hannover: 2005.

Herlihy, David. *Opera Muliebria: Women and Work in Medieval Europe.* Philadelphia: 1990.

Hoffman, Adina and Peter Cole. *Sacred Trash: The Lost and Found World of the Cairo Geniza.* New York: 2011.

Ibn Ganaḥ, Abu al-Walīd Marwān. *Sefer ha-Shorashim, Wurzelwörterbuch der Hebräischen Sprache, von Abulwalîd Merwân ibn Gānāḥ.* Edited by W. Bacher. Berlin: 1896.

Ibn Yaḥya, Gedalyah. *Shalshelet ha-kabbalah.* Venice: 1587.

Jellinek, Adolph. *Bet ha-Midrasch; Sammlung Kleiner Midraschim*, vol. III. Leipzig: 1853.

Jordan, William Chester. *The French Monarchy and the Jews: From Philip Augustus to the Last Capetians.* Philadelphia: 1989.

Kadari, Adiel. "'All Drink from the Same Fountain': The Initial Acceptance of the Halakhot of Eldad Ha-Dani into the Halakhic Discourse." *Review of Rabbinic Judaism* 13/2 (2010), 211–228.

Kadari, Adiel. "On Accepting the 'Other' and its Limitations: A Study of the Gaon R. Zemaḥ's Responsa on the Matter of Eldad the Danite." In Uri Ehrlich, Howard Kreisel, and Daniel J. Lasker, eds., *By the Well: Studies in Jewish Philosophy and Halakhic Thought Presented to Gerald Blidstein.* Beer Sheva: 2008, 449–461 [Hebrew].

Kahen, Hasamein Wasef. *Samaritan History, Identity, Religion and Subdivisions, Literature and Social Status.* Jerusalem: 1966.

Kaplan, Steven. "A Note on the Hebrew Letters of Prester John." *Journal of Jewish Studies* 36/2 (1985): 230–234.

Kaplan, Steven. *The Beta Israel (Falasha) in Ethiopia: From Earliest Times to the Twentieth Century.* New York and London: 1992.

Knefelkamp, Ulrich. "Der Priesterkönig Johannes und sein Reich – Legende oder Realität." *Journal of Medieval History* 14 (1988): 337–355.

Kokovtsov, Pavel K. *Hebrew-Khazarian Correspondence of the Xth Century* (=Павел К. Кёкёвцёв, *Еврейскё-хазарская переписка в X веке*). Leningrad: 1932.

Kosman, Admiel. "The Aggadah about the Conflict between Adam and the Angels over the Naming of the Animals according to the Eldad ha-Dani Version." *Mo'ed* 13 (2003): 79–88 [Hebrew].

Krauss, Samuel. "New Light on Geographical Information of Eldad Hadani and Benjamin of Tudela." *Tarbiẓ* 8 (1936), 208–232 [Hebrew].

Linder, Amnon. *The Jews in Roman Imperial Legislation.* Detroit and Jerusalem: 1987.

Linder, Amnon. *The Jews in the Legal Sources of the Early Middle Ages.* Detroit: 1997.

Lowes, John L. "The Dry Sea and the Carrenare." *Modern Philology* 3/1 (1905): 9–19.

Luzzatto, Philoxéne. *Mémoire sur les Juifs d'Abyssinie ou Falashas.* Extrait des Archives Israélites. Paris: 1852.

Mack, Hannanel. *The Mystery of Rabbi Moshe Hadarshan.* Jerusalem: 2010 [Hebrew].

Mann, Jacob. *Text and Studies in Jewish History and Literature*, 2 vols. Cincinnati: 1931.

Margulies, Mordechai. *Land of Israel Halakhas from the Geniza*. Jerusalem: 1973 [Hebrew].

Matthew Paris's English History: From the Year 1235 to 1273. Translated by John A. Giles. London: 1852.

Menache, Sophia. "Matthew Paris's Attitudes Toward Anglo-Jewry." *Journal of Medieval History* 23/2 (1997): 139–162.

Menache, Sophia. "Tartars, Jews, Saracens and the Jewish-Mongol 'Plot' of 1241." *History* 81 (1996): 319–342.

Morag, Shlomo. "Eldad Haddani's Hebrew and the Problem of his Provenance." *Tarbiẓ* 66 (1997): 223–246 [Hebrew].

Müller, David Heinrich. *Die Recensionen und Versionen des Eldad had-Dânî*. Vienna: 1892.

Nahoum, Haïm. "Mission chez les Falachas d'Abyssinie." *Bulletin de l'Alliance israélite universelle* 33/3 (1908): 100–137.

[Nathan ben Jehiel]. *Sefer ha-arukh*. Edited by Salomon Buber, facsimile of the 1888 edition. Jerusalem: 1978 [Hebrew].

Neubauer, Adolf. "Sources relating the Ten Tribes." *Kobez al Jad* (*Sammelband Kleiner Beiträge aus Handschriften*) IV (1888): 8–74 [Hebrew].

Neubauer, Adolf. "Where are the Ten Lost Tribes, II – Eldad the Danite." *JQR* 1 (1889): 95–144.

Nisse, Ruth. "A Romance of the Jewish East: The Ten Lost Tribes and The Testaments of the Twelve Patriarchs in Medieval Europe." *Medieval Encounters* 13 (2007): 499–523.

Nowell, Charles E. "The Historical Prester John." *Speculum* 28/3 (1953): 435–445.

Parfitt, Tudor. "Construction of Jewish Identities in Africa." In Parfitt and Emanuela Trevisan Semi, *Jews of Ethiopia: The Birth of an Elite*. London and New York: 2005.

Patschovsky, Alexander. *Der Passauer Anonymus: Ein Sammelwerk über Ketzer, Juden, Antichrist aus der Mitte des 13. Jahrhunderts*. Stuttgart: 1968.

Perry, Micha J. "Female Soḥatot: Tradition, Law and Reality at the end of the Middle Ages." In E. Baumgarten et al., eds., *Tov Elem: Memory, Community and Gender in Medieval and Early Modern Jewish Societies. Essays in Honor of Robert Bonfil*. Jerusalem: 2011, 127–146 [Hebrew].

Perry, Micha J. "The Imaginary War between Prester John and Eldad the Danite and Its Real Implications." *Viator* 41/1 (2010): 5–10.

Perry, Micha J. *Tradition and Transformation: Knowledge Transmission among European Jews in the Middle Ages*. Bnei Brak: 2010 [Hebrew].

Polliack, Meira. *Karaite Judaism: A Guide to its History and Literary Sources*. Leiden – Boston: 2003.

Poznański, Abraham. "Compilations from Sefer megilat starim by Our Rabbi Nissim ben R. Jacob of Kairouan." *Ha-tzofeh le-ḥokhmat Yisrael*, vol. vii (1923) [Hebrew].

Ramos, Manuel João. *Essays in Christian Mythology: The Metamorphosis of Prester John.* New York, Toronto, and Oxford: 2006.

Régné, Jean. *History of the Jews in Aragon: Regesta and Documents, 1213–1327.* Edited by Yom Tov Assis. Jerusalem: 1978.

Rosen, Tova. "Kazahrs, Mongols, and the Pains of the Time of Messiah." In Michal Oron, ed., *Between History and Literature.* Tel Aviv: 1983, 42–59 [Hebrew].

Roth, Norman. "Eldad Ha-Daniy (The Danite)." In Norman Roth, ed., *Medieval Jewish Civilization: An Encyclopedia.* New York and London: 2003, 238b-240a.

Roth, Norman. "Review of The Hebrew Letters of Prester John, eds. Edward Ullendorff and C. F. Beckingham." *Hebrew Studies* 25 (1984): 192–195.

Scheiber, Alexander. "Eléments fabuleux dans l'Eshkôl Hakôfer de Juda Hadasi." *REJ* 108 (1948): 41–62.

Schirmann, Jefim (Haim). *Hebrew Poetry in Spain and Provençe,* 2 vols. Jerusalem: 1961 [Hebrew].

Schloessinger, Max. *The Ritual of Eldad ha-Dani.* Leipzig and New York: 1908.

Schmieder, Felicitas. "Christians, Jews, Muslims – and Mongols: Fitting a Foreign People into the Western Christian Apocalyptic Scenario." *Medieval Encounters* 12/2 (2006): 274–295.

Schmitt, Jean-Claude. *The Conversion of Herman the Jew: Autobiography, History and Fiction in the Twelfth Century.* Translated by Alex J. Novikoff. Philadelphia: 2010.

Schur, Nathan. *History of the Karaites.* Jerusalem: 2003 [Hebrew].

Sefer Eldad ha-Dani. Mantua: 1480.

Sefer nitzahon yashan [The Book of an Old Triumph]. Philadelphia: 1976.

Seligsohn, M. "Sambation." *Jewish Encyclopedia.* 1906.

Silverstein, Adam. "From Markets to Marvels: Jews on the Maritime Route to China ca. 850-ca. 950 CE." *Journal of Jewish Studies* 58/1 (Spring 2007): 91–104.

Simonson, Shlomo. *The Apostolic See and the Jews,* vol. VII: History. Toronto: 1991.

Slush, David. *May the Outcast of Israel Assemble: On Ethiopian Jewry.* Jerusalem: 1988 [Hebrew].

Soloveitchik, Haym. *Collected Essays,* vol. II. Oxford and Portland, OR: 2014.

Soloveitchik, Haym. *Halakha, Economy, and Self-Image.* Jerusalem: 1985 [Hebrew].

Soloveitchik, Haym. "Rupture and Reconstruction: The Transformation of Contemporary Orthodoxy." *Tradition* 28/4 (1994): 64–130.

Soloveitchik, Haym. "Three Themes in Sefer Hasidim." *AJS Review* 1 (1976): 311–357.

Sperber, Daniel. *Minhagei Yisrael: Origins and History,* vol. IV. Jerusalem: 1995 [Hebrew].

Stein Kokin, Daniel. "Toward the Source of the Sambatyon: Shabbat Discourse and the Origins of the Sabbatical River Legend." *AJS Review* 37 (2013): 1–28.

Stow, Kenneth R. "Reviewed Work: The Hebrew Letters of Prester John by Edward Ullendorff and Charles F. Beckingham." *Speculum* 59 (1984): 447–449.

Sussmann, Jacob. "The Ashkenazi Yerushalmi MS — 'Sefer Yerushalmi'." *Tarbiẓ* 66/1 (1995): 37–63 [Hebrew].

Sussman, Jacob. "The Oral Law as Simple as it Sounds: The Power of the Tip of a Yud." In Jacob Sussman and David Rosenthal, eds. *Meḥqerei Talmud*, vol. 3/1. Jerusalem:2005, 209–384 [Hebrew].

Ta-Shma, Israel Moshe, *Early Franco-German Ritual and Custom*. Revised third edition. Jerusalem: 1999 [Hebrew].

Ta-Shma, Israel Moshe. "On Some Franco-German Nidda Practices." *Sidra* 9 (1993): 164–170 [Hebrew].

Ta-Shma, Israel Moshe. *Ritual, Custom and Reality in Franco-Germany, 1000–1350*. Jerusalem: 1996 [Hebrew].

Ta-Shma, Israel Moshe. *Talmudic Commentary in Europe and North Africa: Literary History*, first part: 1000–1200. Revised second edition. Jerusalem: 1999 [Hebrew].

Turner, James. *Philology: The Forgotten Origins of the Modern Humanities*. Princeton: 2014.

Ullendorff, Edward and Charles F. Beckingham. *The Hebrew Letters of Prester John*. Oxford: 1982.

Valdman, Menachem. *Beyond the Rivers of Ethiopia*. Tel Aviv: 1989 [Hebrew].

Valdman, Menachem. "Marriage and Divorce among Ethiopian Jewry." *Teḥumin* 11 (1990): 214–240 [Hebrew].

Voß, Rebekka. *Umstrittene Erlöser. Politik, Ideologie und jüdisch-christlicher Messianismus in Deutschland, 1500–1600*. Göttingen: 2011.

Wagner, Bettina. *Die 'Epistola presbiteri Johannis' lateinisch und deutsch: Überlieferung, Textgeschichte, Rezeption und Übertragungen im Mittelalter*. Tübingen: 2000.

Wasserstein, David J. "Eldad ha-Dani and Prester John." In Charles F. Beckingham and Bernard Hamilton, eds. *Prester John, the Mongols and the Ten Lost Tribes*. Aldershot, Hampshire: 1996, 213–236.

Yuval, Israel Jacob. "Jewish Messianic Expectations towards 1240 and Christian Reactions." In Peter Schäfer and Mark Cohen, eds. *Toward the Millennium – Messianic Expectations from the Bible to Waco*. Leiden: 1998, 105–121.

Yuval, Israel Jacob. *Two Nations in Your Womb: Perceptions of Jews and Christians in Late Antiquity and the Middle Ages*. Translated by Barbara Harshav and Jonathan Chipman. Berkeley: 2006.

Zaldes, Nadia. "A Magical Event in Sicily: Notes and Clarifications on the Messianic Movement in Sicily." *Zion* 58/3 (1993): 347–363 [Hebrew].

Zarncke, Friedrich. *Der Priester Johannes*, 2 vols. Leipzig: 1876–1879.

Zuriely, Yosef. "Permission for Women to Slaughter: A Safeguard within a Safeguard." *Hagigai Giv'ah* 3 (1995): 91–99 [Hebrew].

Zuriely, Yosef. "Ritual Sheḥita by Women: Halakha and Practice." *Proceedings of the World Congress of Jewish Studies* II (division C, 1993): 169–176 [Hebrew].

Zuriely, Yosef. "Slaughtering Approvals for Women." In Joseph Dahuh Halevi, ed. *Mabuei Afikim*. Tel Aviv: 1995, 313–323 [Hebrew].

Index

Taylor & Francis eBooks

www.taylorfrancis.com

A single destination for eBooks from Taylor & Francis
with increased functionality and an improved user
experience to meet the needs of our customers.

90,000+ eBooks of award-winning academic content in
Humanities, Social Science, Science, Technology, Engineering,
and Medical written by a global network of editors and authors.

TAYLOR & FRANCIS EBOOKS OFFERS:

A streamlined
experience for
our library
customers

A single point
of discovery
for all of our
eBook content

Improved
search and
discovery of
content at both
book and
chapter level

REQUEST A FREE TRIAL
support@taylorfrancis.com

 Routledge
Taylor & Francis Group

 CRC Press
Taylor & Francis Group